The 8-Lane
Highway

The 8-Lane Highway

DANNY L. FORMHALS SR.

authorHOUSE®

AuthorHouse™ LLC
1663 Liberty Drive
Bloomington, IN 47403
www.authorhouse.com
Phone: 1-800-839-8640

Published by AuthorHouse   06/19/2014

ISBN: 978-1-4969-2119-2 (sc)
ISBN: 978-1-4969-2120-8 (e)

Table of Contents

WARNING!!!

This book is a warning call from one
watchman standing on the wall.
To our nation, to our churches and to believers

This warning is written to the
three kinds of believers:
(1) The true followers of Christ
(2) The lukewarm followers
(3) The fallen away ones

JUDGEMENT IS COMING!

About the Author

Danny Formhals Sr. was saved at the age of eight while attending Northeast Assembly of God in Fresno, CA. In his sophomore year of High School he began attending The Peoples Church, where he was greatly influenced and felt God's call to full-time ministry. He began attending Bethany University, and graduated with a degree in church leadership in 1993.

After 15 years of full-time youth ministry, it was time for another step of faith. That step of faith led to an expansion of their ministry as they traveled throughout the west coast in full-time evangelism; singing, preaching and using drama to share God's Word.

In January 2005 Danny, Michele, and their two children were invited to Pastor Abundant Life Center in McKinleyville, California where they live now. Danny currently serves on the Redwood Teen Challenge board, the Redwood Family Camp board, and serves as the Redwood Section Presbyter for the Northern California/Nevada District of the Assemblies of God.

Danny has written several books, Bible studies, and devotionals; including his most recent book, Moments of Truth (Three Things Every Christian Should Know).

DEDICATION and CHALLENGE

To: Pastors, Ministers and God's People

This book is dedicated to every pastor, minister, and believer serving the Lord in the local church. Thank you for loving and caring for God's people. If I could, I would tell you in person that I love you in the Lord. Your job isn't easy as you serve on the front lines of God's army. My hope is that this book will challenge your thinking about the condition of the Christian community, and inspire you to warn the people that Jesus is coming soon. This book will stir you up and you may struggle with some of the things I bring out. With your Bible in hand, an open heart and mind, you might just see what I see.

I WROTE THIS BOOK in the Spirit of L.O.V.E.:

(L) **In the Spirit of LOVE** – *"Let all that you do be done with love"* (1 Cor. 16:14), because *"God is love"* (1 John 4:8).

(O) To challenge you, knowing that **some might get OFFENDED** – "Offenses will certainly come" (Luke 17:1 _{HCSB}).

(V) Because w**e are VICTORIOUS** when we know the truth – *"Your Word is truth"* (John 17:17), and *"The entirety of Your* word is truth, And every one of Your righteous judgments endures forever" (Ps. 119:160).

(E) **The real ENEMY is not each another,** but Satan and His demons – *"For we do not wrestle against flesh and blood, but against principalities, against powers, against the rulers of the darkness of this age, against spiritual hosts of wickedness in the heavenly places"* (Eph. 6:12), and because *"He is a liar and the father of it"* (John 8:44).

Your fellow worker in Christ,
Danny Formhals Sr.

INTRODUCTION

I love the local church. It is the HOPE for the city. Each pastor, member and attender has a tremendous responsibility. Their directive is to reach their perspective communities with the gospel to win the lost and disciple the believer. The Bible is jam-packed with various mandates given to the local church and the individual within. Before and after Jesus ascended He left the disciples with some specific ones. It is important to note: They were His direct words to the founders of the early church. Therefore, each local church has this mandate as well:

- To make disciples (Matt. 28:19).
- To baptize them (Matt. 28:19).
- To preach the gospel (Mark 16:15).
- To wait for the promise (Acts 1:4).

I wrote this book because the local church is hurting. In cities and towns all across our great land, the local church (which is the Body of Christ) struggles. They want to make a difference, yet it's just not happening. All churches wax and wane in attendance, but most growth isn't due solely to new converts. One pastor, said, "70% of church growth is transfer growth." Transfer growth is people hopping from one church to another. It breaks the heart of God when churches in the same city compete to have the best Sunday morning service experience, instead of winning the lost. Even though some good things are happening out there, the ineffective church is becoming the norm. They lack the vision, the people and the resources in order to make a difference. Pastors cry out for help, but few show up. Pastor's call for prayer and only a small handful come. Still others are too wounded to get involved. Something is terribly wrong and things need to change. A Holy Ghost revival is our greatest need. Pastor John Hagee said, "We don't need revival in the White House, we need revival in the church!" The few churches experiencing revival are blessed. Others want it, but don't have it. Sadly, most don't want it. Without the power and presence of the Holy Spirit, the local church is doomed.

The local church struggles because of internal conflicts. Every church has its faithful, strong, and committed; those alive in Christ. Many in the battle have fallen. The Christian community is being torn apart from within. Today, many who call themselves Christians are either deceived or ignorant to what God is looking for. They lack a love for the Word of God, they have fallen asleep spiritually (2 Thess. 2). Overall; the church has lost her voice. We are running out of time because Jesus is coming back (John 14:28). This book is like the letter King Hezekiah sent to the people of his kingdom. They were in trouble. I see the runners going out all across the nation, with the *"shout of the Lord"* and a message from the King.

> *Then the runners went throughout all Israel and Judah with the letters*
> *from the king and his leaders, and spoke according to the command*
> *of the king: "Children of Israel, **return to the Lord** God of Abraham,*
> *Isaac, and Israel; then He will return to the remnant of you who have*

*escaped from the hand of the kings of Assyria. ⁷And do not be like your fathers and your brethren, who trespassed against the Lord God of their fathers, so that He gave them up to desolation, as you see. ⁸Now do not be stiff-necked, as your fathers were, but yield yourselves to the Lord; and enter His sanctuary, which He has sanctified forever, and serve the Lord your God, that the fierceness of His wrath may turn away from you. ⁹For if you **return to the Lord**, your brethren and your children will be treated with compassion by those who lead them captive, so that they may come back to this land; for the Lord your God is gracious and merciful, and will not turn His face from you if you **return to Him**"* -2 Chronicles 30:6-9 (emphasis mine)

Our Great King Jesus is sending His runners, throughout the land to every community and church. His message hasn't changed. He said, *"It's time to Return to Me."* When individuals yield to Him and follow hard after his Word, His blessings will follow. If the local church and its leaders get back to the basic mandates, His presence will absolutely come. If our nation repents of its sinful ways and returns to the Lord, *"He will heal our land"* (2 Chron. 7:14).

Nine years ago I came to a small town in Northern California. I came with a strong desire to see revival, a promise that God will soon fulfill. The church I currently pastor has ebbed and flowed. It has become evident the Christian culture has shifted in the wrong direction. In our decline, our passion for Jesus has become a passion for the things of the world, pleasure, and self.

THIS BOOK IS A WAKE UP CALL TO EVERYONE WHO CLAIMS TO LOVE THE LORD JESUS. This book is a strong warning to:

- **Pastors** – You must know the Word and preach ALL of it with conviction. The Word is what saves.

- **Christians** – You must study the Word, or you will be deceived by Satan. You must get involved.
- **Local churches** – To make a lasting impact, a Holy Ghost revival is our greatest hope. Get to together and pray for the presence of God to come again.
- **Religions/Religious groups** – If you have strayed from the Word of God, get back to the founding Biblical principles. People need Jesus not religion.
- **The Lost Person** – You are the target because Jesus loves you. Open your heart to Him today.
- **Politicians** – Almighty God placed you in office (Rom. 13:1) to represent the people. One day everything will be brought into the open (Luke 8:17).
- **Fathers** – You are the key to a spiritually healthy home (Psalm 78:1-8). Be a man of God for your wife and children. God's way is the best way.
- **Parents** – Stay married if you can; statistically it's better for your children. Put God first and your children will follow. Train them to serve the Lord (Prov. 22:6).
- **Reporters/News Networks** – Deceiving the masses is wrong. Tell the truth because God's judgment is coming. One day, God will reveal the things done in secret (Mark 4:22).

To everyone – God's Judgment is coming.
IT'S TIME TO RETURN TO THE LORD!

Chapter 1 – We're losing our Voice

"It may not always be easy, convenient, or politically correct to stand for truth and right, but it is the right thing to do...always." –M. Russell Ballard

Our Politically Correct Society

Words are powerful, but God's Word is unstoppable. The enemy of our soul, Satan continues his all-out assault on twisting God's Word and attacking God's people. There is much controversy about what people should and shouldn't do or say in our culture. In stark contrast of the First Amendment to the United States Constitution, assuring us the right to free speech, it is becoming more and more taboo to speak out freely. This will continue to escalate, especially for believers. Today quoting from the Bible is offensive to many, and one day will be a punishable offense; even considered a hate crime. In the future many Bible believers will be arrested, prosecuted and imprisoned for what they adhere to and believe in. Books like this one will be burned and confiscated. Throughout history, as in Nazi Germany, the Middle Ages, and early church history; the mass eradication of books did occur. If we haven't learned from the past, we are doomed to repeat it.

From the Duck Dynasty controversial comment, concerning the gay and lesbian movement, to the war on Christmas and the Cross, free speech has morphed into free speech with an asterisk.

To some, what the Bible calls sin is frowned upon like screaming "fire" in a crowded theater. Believers in Christ and His Word are suffering from spiritual laryngitis. I use the word Christian instead of believer because; "Christian" has changed from its original meaning over the years. A cultural war rages for the loudest and most persistent voice. Evil and darkness are winning more and more battles. Those who oppose the Biblical viewpoint and claim to be tolerant are often hypocritical in their attempts to quiet truth. Bible believers are looked down upon when they speak out from the scriptures. This is clear many have forgotten or don't believe our nation was founded upon Biblical principals in the Word of God.

Will the real bigots and intolerant please stand up? In reality, it's the Lord who is tolerant. He continues to love, forgive and accept despite our sinful ways. It will be our cold, unrepentant and hardened hearts that will bring God's judgment. We can't forget nor dismiss that God is God and sin is sin. Our blatant disregard for God and His Word has led to a free-fall in morality. The moral decline of America, is gaining steam. So down the proverbial rabbit hole we go; to who knows where. Once it's all said and done, history will prove again that *"For lack of guidance a nation falls"* (Prov. 11:14 NIV), and *"A nation without God's guidance is a nation without order"* (Prov. 29:18 GNTA). If we continue to thumb our nose at God and His Word, the greatest nation on earth will go the way of the Greek, Assyrian and Roman Empires. The Bible says, *"Blessed is the nation whose God is the Lord"* (Ps. 33:12).

We must continue to speak out against the moral decline of our nation. A resent Pew Research Study said, "Millennial's (18-33 years old) are the least religious generation." The big question is who will be brave enough to speak out? Who will hide and shun their responsibility in Christ? Who will be a witness or a wimp; a real Christian or a coward? It amazes me how many don't believe a time of serious persecution is coming to the church in America. To imagine a preacher, anyone for that matter, arrested and charged with a hate-crime for quoting certain passages from the Bible seems far-fetched right? Not so. The Jews in Hitler's Germany were abruptly ripped from their homes and families to suffer and die in concentration camps. Still don't believe men and women of God can be hauled away in America for speaking against the politically correct, "PC" society? Ask the shocked and perplexed American Japanese as they were unexpectedly rushed into internment camps after Japan attacked Pearl Harbor on December 7, 1941. This and much more chaos is right around the corner. Just pick up the Bible and you'll see that Jesus is literally *"At the door"* (Rev. 3:20), and judgment is soon to follow.

Silence isn't golden

There is a time for quiet, but now is not that time. One of the purposes of this book is to embolden believers to never relent their voice for God. In Matthew's gospel Jesus is speaking about the Kingdom of God, which is a relationship with Christ. He says, *"The kingdom of heaven suffers violence, and the violent take it by force"* (Matt.

11:12). Now is the time for the army of God to stand up and make a difference. Not enough of us are bravely affirming what the Bible has been saying for thousands of years. This is a sign we're in trouble. When political correctness keeps biblical principles and guidelines in check, this nation suffers. To lose our voice now would be disastrous for individuals and families. The decline of the family structure is proof of the overall failure of the church and its attenders to *"Preach the Word"* (2 Tim. 4:2). According to *The Telegraph*, "The proportion of children born to unmarried mothers hit a record 47.5 percent in 2012." If things continue, many believe, by 2016 more children will be born out of wedlock than in married households. While ultimately, God's Word will endure forever (1 Peter 1:25), our silence in this culture isn't golden. Kim an old friend recently said, "I am convinced we will go to our graves with words unsaid in an effort to be appropriate or polite." We must be ready a willing to use our mouths to say, in the spirit of love, what must be said; especially when God fills our mouths with His Words.

Time to shout

There is a power in being loud. I once heard an old musician say, "Loud is the will of God." If you listen, which voice is trumping the other; the secular or the believer? In Jeremiah 50 the wrath of the Lord is being poured out against Babylon. The people were instructed to *"Shout against her all around"* (Jer. 50:14-15) because she had sinned against the Lord. We must understand that evil and sin will lose its power if we raise our voices against it. This must happen both in our churches and in our nation.

In Joshua 6 Israel was about to conquer its first city in the Promised Land. Jericho, a very powerful city was to be dedicated to the Lord. It was a first fruit offering unto the Lord. The people were instructed to keep nothing for themselves. Absolutely nothing! Only Rahab and her family would be spared because she helped the spies by hiding them (Joshua 6:17). When the trumpet sounded, the people were told to shout. Here's what happened next, *"So the people shouted when the priests blew the trumpets. And it happened when the people heard the sound of the trumpet, and the people shouted with a great shout, that the wall fell down flat. Then the people went up into the city, every man straight before him, and they took the city"* (Joshua 6:20). I can only imagine the incredible spiritual walls that would fall in America if we could come together in cities, towns and communities. If we shout together we may witness the next Holy Spirit revival come and shake us. It's time to rise up and S.H.O.U.T.:

S – (SEE) the city as Jesus does. Luke 19:41 *"Now as He drew near, He saw the city and wept over it."* We must have a burden (broken hearts) for the community, the business, the families, and the people.

H – Cry out to the (HOLY SPIRIT) for revival. Prayer is the single most important element to reaching your city for Christ.

O – Become an (OUTREACH) driven church. The focus must be on sharing the gospel message in the spirit of love, to the lost.

U – Call people to (UNITE). People need a cause and vision to become motivated. There is strength in numbers.

T – It's going to take a (TEAM). Not one church, not one pastor, but many coming together in the spirit of cooperation. Partnering together will be challenging, but try anyway.

Unity or Bust

God used the shout of unison to rally the people and demolish walls. Today, believers can't agree on much. In my city, I've seen this first hand. We say we're one, but we're so far from a shout of unity. One day I was having a discussion with someone in my community that had a strong ministry, but didn't want to commit to a local church. He had the same sincere heart and passion for the Lord as I did. For the first time as a pastor, I literally pleaded with him to come and join me in my church, because he didn't have one. He continued to resist because he'd been hurt before. He thought he could thrive without the local church; which is the Body of Christ. We were so close to connecting, but just couldn't agree. Then the Lord spoke this to my heart, "You two are in the same book, just not on the same page." This has become the plight of many smaller churches. They're often left without ministry and many solo ministers are left without God's covering.

Satan's plan to divide has been one of his best strategies. The Message Bible says, *"Do two people walk hand in hand if they aren't going to the same place?"* (Amos 3:3). Unfortunately, good people with their own agenda can cause strong divisions in the local church. Paul warns Titus about such people, and how to deal with them. In Titus 3:10-11 he says, *"If people are causing divisions among you, give a first and second warning. After that, have nothing more to do with them. For people like that have turned away from the truth, and their own sins condemn them."* Paul teaches that those who cause division do so for two reasons. First, they have turned away from the truth. In many circumstances good people try and do things their own way, and not the Lord's way. Paul refers to them as "Turning away from truth." This is important because *truth* is the Word of God. We can expect unbelievers to reject the truth in part or in whole, but not believers. When God's people undermine and go around God's established Biblical order they are wrong. Pastors aren't perfect, but they are called to lead their churches in spite of their imperfections, to find *"Faithful people"* (2 Tim. 2:2) to come along beside them. Those who try and go over their spiritual leaders or go around them end up causing division. The truth is, the Word of God gives pastors the Biblical authority to lead and equip people (Eph. 4:11), not the other way around. While many hands make light work, too many cooks in the kitchen spoil the broth. People need to allow their spiritual leaders lead them and to purpose in their heart to walk with them.

The second thing Paul says about those who cause division is that it is due to their own sins. These people are condemned by their own arguments. Many Christians today want to argue with their leaders about common things; such to what a pastor should or shouldn't do. Often the topics include things clearly outlined in scripture. It is one thing to ask questions, it is another to know better than God's Word. Paul exhorts Titus after the second argument to *"Have nothing to do with them."* The Jamieson-Fausset-Brown Bible Commentary says about them, "He cannot say, no one told him better: continuing the same after frequent admonition, he is self-condemned. He sinneth wilfully against knowledge." Here are some various modern translations of Titus 3:11: (1) God's Word (GW) says, *"You know that people like this are corrupt. They are sinners condemned by their own actions."* (2) The Message (MSG) says, *"It's obvious that such a person is out of line, rebellious against God. By persisting in divisiveness he cuts himself off."* (3) The New International Version (NIV) says, *"You may be sure that such a man is warped and sinful; he is self-condemned."* (4) The Amplified says, *"Well aware that such a person has utterly changed (is perverted and corrupted); he goes on sinning [though he] is convicted of guilt and self-condemned."* (5) The New Living Testament (NLT) says, *"For people like that have turned away from the truth, and their own sins condemn them."* (6) The Holman Christian Standard Bible (HCSB) says, *"Knowing that such a person is perverted and sins, being self-condemned."*

For a variety of reasons and faulty beliefs Christians can't walk in agreement, or they have different destinations. All the while the Bible screams, unity and purpose. The Body of Christ is the local churches, not individuals or ministries. Christ is the head and the church is the Body of Christ. The local church is the place for the gifts of the Holy Spirit. Speaking to the church in Corinth, Paul says, *"Now you are the body of Christ, and members individually"* (1 Cor. 12:27). The hand is not the body; it is a part of the Body. To our discredit, the local church has ceased doing the ministry as the early church did. Without a spirit of cooperation and unity in the Body of Christ, the church will fail to win the lost. Too many local churches, especially the smaller ones are having a hard go of it because of division.

> *For a variety of reasons and faulty beliefs Christians can't walk in agreement, or they have different destinations.*

Rarely do good intentions translate into actions. To their demise, many ministers and Christians think they know better than God's Word. Instead, of walking in agreement we argue about pews and padded chairs, the color of the sanctuary carpet and watch good people walk out the doors of the local church to do ministry alone. On a greater scale our failure to recognize division leaves us weakened. Therefore, we stand idly by as corrupt politicians and liberal judges give away our rights. Christianity has lost many battles because we lack harmony. We have failed with issues like abortion, prayer in schools, and the constant challenges facing our "Freedom of religion" assurances in the First Amendment to the United States Constitution. The lack of unity has become, without a doubt a serious problem. *"Where there is no vision, the people perish"* (Prov. 29:18 ₖⱼᵥ), so Christian voice will continue to be pushed around at the ballot box and in the world. Have we become like David who said, *"Is there not a cause?"* (1 Sam. 17:29).

Who will stand up and shout, "Lord, give us the city?" Who is willing to fight for a nation, a city, a community, a family, and an individual? If we could unite as one, we would win the day for the glory of God. Take a moment and listen. Do you hear a battle cry, or do the crickets still own the night? We MUST fight for the Word of God; which is being abused, abandoned, and attacked. It's time to pull the duct tape off our mouths. It seems as though I'm preaching to the choir and sadly, in many churches the choir isn't even showing up. Let's be passionate to see that God's Word has its day again. Only God's Word can give a broken, hurting heart a chance. Only Jesus, the Word that became flesh, can truly change lives. After all, He is *"The Way, the Truth, and the Life"* (John 14:6). However, if we don't open our mouths and speak up in the spirit of unity, "There is no way, the truth will come out and change a Life."

The voice of a Champion

Did you know you are greatly desired of the Lord? Make no mistake about it; let no one tell you differently, your Heavenly Father has moved heaven and earth to win your heart. Jesus said, *"I came to give life"* (John 10:10). He wants you for His own, so Jesus paid the ultimate price and died for you. God not only wants to give you life, but life with a greater purpose. His requirement is a living heart, one that is fully and completely His (2 Chron. 16:9). He knows a heart which beats for Him will *"Go into the entire world and preach the Gospel"* (Mark 16:15). Like the early disciples, nothing will stop you from raising your voice for the cause of Christ.

Champions have confidence when they face an opponent. They know why they are in the ring, on the field, and in the game. They know their purpose, and why they exist. Dr. John C. Maxwell said, "Over the years as I have watched and listened to successful people, I have discovered a common thread; they know WHY they're here. Knowing their purpose in life gives them stability. Someone once said there are two great days in life—the day you are born and the day you discover WHY."

God is looking for a champion with a voice. St. Teresa of Avila said, "Christ has no hands but yours. Christ has no eyes but yours. Christ has no feet but yours. Christ has no body on Earth but yours." I would like to add one more line to St. Teresa's words, "Christ has no voice on Earth but yours." When did Christians stop speaking up? Our loved ones and neighbors need to be told, *"Repent of your sins and turn to God"* (Matt. 3:2). When did the message of the cross go from hearts and mouths to some remote place in us? Who in history made the decision to be silent? The stillness in the Christian community is an invitation to stray off of God's path. Today, too many good people are merging onto the wrong path. Once we stop telling the world about God's love and His Word the only path that remains is a road toward death and destruction. God wants to put a powerful two-edge sword in the hands of a champion. You are his warrior and sword bearer.

"For the word of God is living and powerful, and sharper than any two-edged sword, piercing even to the division of soul and spirit, and of joints and marrow, and is a discerner of the thoughts and intents of the heart" – Hebrews 4:12

The Bible is called the Word for a Reason

The purpose of the gospel was to be announced to the whole world, *"Then the end will come"* (Matt. 24:14). The Bible is God's Word, and words don't have power unless they are spoken and heard. The Word is powerful, not merely words on a page. They are living and breathing. Millions upon millions have been changed by them. GOD'S WORD IS ALIVE! It was given to show all of us a better, stronger life, and to prepare us for heaven. It was entrusted to us; to make a difference in people? *"All Scripture is God-breathed and is useful for correcting, rebuking, encouraging, and for training in righteousness"* (2 Tim. 3:16). To simply hear it and read it generates greater faith. Romans 10:17 states, *"Faith comes by hearing, and hearing by the Word of God."* I like how the Amplified states it, *"So faith comes by hearing [what is told], and what is heard comes by the preaching [of the message that came from the lips] of Christ (the Messiah Himself)."*

A little bit of the spoken Word has tremendous potential to change any horrible situation. Yet, if believers remain silent; sin, death and condemnation will fill the void. *"Sin is crouching at the door"* (Gen. 4:7), and silence guarantees failure in the short term. Eighteen times the Bible says, *"He who has an ear, let him hear."* All but one time, the Lord is speaking. God left us with the message the world needs to hear. Jesus said in Matthew 13:43, *"Then the righteous will shine forth as the sun in the kingdom of their Father. He who has ears to hear, let him hear!"* The time has come for the local church to open its mouth and speak and give people an opportunity to HEAR. It's time for *"Those who are upright and in right standing with God"* (Job 17:9 ₐₘₚ) to shine for Christ in the Father's Kingdom.

Christian Introverts

How can people believe and follow Christ when all they hear is silence? If we don't teach, preach and live the truth; lies and deception will fill the void. If we don't speak out Christian introverts will continue to rule the local church. Soon, we will have no say, no voice, and no power. In his article *The Christian Introvert*, Tim Challies said, "I have no right to crave introverted solitude. Rather, the gospel compels me to deny even that trait and all its desires in order to serve other people. I am introverted, but this does not give me a different calling in life than the gregarious Christian." The hope for America is growing darker. Right now, in the neighborhoods of our land, the life God's Word offers is threatened like at no other time in history. The wrong champions are rising up all the time. They are fighting to destroy God's plan, His Word and His people. It's time for the spirit of David to rise up in us. The armies of the living God need another shepherd boy to step onto the battle field and face the goliaths of today. David had the spirit of God upon him. We must follow his example.

- **David spoke to the soldiers,** *"For who is this uncircumcised Philistine that he should defy the armies of the living God?"*

(1 Sam. 17:26). We must **speak to the soldiers** in the Lord's army. We must encourage them, give them confidence and remind them whom they serve.

- **David spoke to the king,** *"David said, The Lord Who delivered me out of the paw of the lion and out of the paw of the bear, He will deliver me out of the hand of this Philistine. And Saul said to David, Go, and the Lord be with you!"* (1 Sam. 17:37). We must **speak to our King** and get our marching orders.

- **David spoke to the enemy,** *"Then said David to the Philistine, You come to me with a sword, a spear, and a javelin, but I come to you in the name of the Lord of hosts, the God of the ranks of Israel, Whom you have defied. This day the Lord will deliver you into my hand, and I will smite you and cut off your head"* (1 Sam. 17:45-46). We must **speak against the enemy** and all who defy the Word of God, which is Jesus Christ.

Chapter 2 – Making the Right Choice

"I know your works, that you are neither cold nor hot.
I could wish you were cold or hot. So then, because
you are lukewarm, and neither cold nor hot, I will
vomit you out of My mouth" –Revelation 3:15-16

Choose Wisely

I love the *Holy Grail* scene in the movie *Indiana Jones and the Last Crusade*. The Holy Grail is the cup Christ used at the Last Supper. It was believed to have magic powers. The plot was to find its hidden location. The movie peaks in the chamber containing various cups, one of which is the *Holy Grail*. Eternal life would be granted to the one who drinks from the cup. Once the protagonist and antagonist of the movie find their way inside the room, a wise choice is demanded. As in all good dramas, the choice wouldn't be easy. The cups and chalices in the room were many; some expensive and priceless. These were the cups of kings and palaces. Mixed together were modest looking cups. These would adorn simple and common households. Somewhere in the assortment rests the blessed cup. While drinking from it meant immortality, drinking from the wrong cup meant immediate death.

The first man went for the most lavish, royal cup saying with confidence, "Truly, this is the cup of the King of Kings." A moment later, as he lowering the cup from his lips his choice became evident to all. The gruesome scene of a man transforming from flesh to dust was quite the cinematic feat. In a matter of seconds he was gone; a pile of nothingness. The guardian of the room said, "He chose poorly." Now, it was up to Indiana Jones, who needed the cup to heal his dying father. Looking over the table of cups, he held a different perspective than the man before him. He chose the simplest cup saying, "This is the cup of a carpenter." Like the hero in most movies, he got it right and saved his father. While just a movie, the point is; life is full of choices. Some choices will kill you and zap potential from underneath you. Biblically there is a choice that leads to everlasting life and one to eternal destruction. William Jennings Bryan said, "Destiny is not a matter of chance; it is a matter of choice." How you live for Christ is a matter of choices. As I see it you have three:

Three Choices for the End-times Church

Choice number one – LIVING FOR JESUS

The first choice is the best choice. This is really the only choice. A follower of Jesus Christ is a serious part of the Kingdom of God. According to S. Michael Houdmann, *"The Kingdom of God embraces all created intelligence, both in heaven and earth that are willingly subject to the Lord and are in fellowship with Him."* Living in the Kingdom is: choosing life over death, Christ or the world, and walking in the Spirit rather than the flesh. It's a matter of being in the world, but not of the world (1 John 2:15-17). Most importantly, living for Jesus is about having a strong, vibrant, and passionate relationship with God's Son. Living for Jesus is the best option out there. It brings the greatest joy, hope and freedom to the individual. Abundant life (John 10:10) within the Kingdom of

God is for those who willfully chose a life of obedience. It doesn't get any clearer than Jesus' own words, *"If you love me you will obey me"* (John 14:15).

While the Bible is a mystery (1 Cor. 2:7) in some ways, it isn't confusing, as some contend. The principals we are called to live by are easy to spot. The Bible is a book that even a child could understand. To understand God's Word it takes a searching, open-minded heart. REAL Christians (not in name only), cannot be ashamed of what the Bible teaches. Jesus taught that the Word of God was truth (John 8:31). You must raise your voice, let your light shine, be involved and *"Always be ready to give an answer for the hope inside you"* (1 Peter 3:15). Matthew 6:33 declares, *"But seek first the kingdom of God and His righteousness, and all these things shall be added to you."* My prayer for this group is, "Lord, put a fire inside them who love you and bring revival to their hearts and churches."

Choice number two – BEING LUKE-WARM

This choice is a dangerous one. Many people, more than we think, fall into this category. My feeling is that 50% percent of those who call themselves Christians have descended into the Luke-warm, not ready for primetime category. I call them *"CINO"* people; **Christian In**

Name Only. This is true because we are living in the end-times and many have fallen away. The Apostle Paul called this the Apostasy (falling away) of the Church" (2 Thess. 2:3). Writer Nathan Jones says, "When we consider that the leading 'evangelical' of our time period is Rob Bell of Mars Hill Church who can write a book that teaches there's no one going to Hell and that God will allow everybody into Heaven and there is no punishment for our rebellion against God, then we know without a shadow of a doubt that the church is in serious, serious trouble."

"I say this in the Spirit of love and Christ"

Let's try some Biblical honesty; God is looking for *"A heart that is fully His"* (2 Chron. 16:9). Not some wishy-washy, half baked, half-hearted man or woman. Today, CINO people love themselves and things more than they love God (2 Tim. 3:1-4). They are often ashamed of the gospel (Rom. 1:16) and unwilling to serve God faithfully (Matt. 24:45-51). They like to leave out certain parts of scripture to suit their sinful choices. They live in ignorance and follow pastors who have ignorant congregations. They like to fix their eyes on Jesus until He says something that doesn't back their watered-down gospel. Then they throw around words like grace and forgiveness, disregarding holiness and obedience. They forget that judgment begins in the house of God (1 Pet. 4:7). Like the Children of Israel, they continually look around and look back toward Egypt and the world and are *"Not fit for the service in the kingdom of God"* (Luke 9:62). Yet, because many don't know their Bibles, let alone read them, CINO people thrive in our society. Because they go unchallenged they continue to pull in the weak and wounded with half-truths and deceptive lies. The only remedy to stop them is another Holy Ghost revival in our land. 2 Timothy

4:3-4 is a clear description of those who are Christians in name only. *"For the time will come when they will not endure sound doctrine, but according to their own desires, because they have itching ears, they will heap up for themselves teachers; and they will turn their ears away from the truth, and be turned aside to fables."* While God wants them hot or cold (not in the middle), they want to hold on to the world, in small ways.

Many Christians fear being radical and beholden to Biblical truths. Have we been reduced to bugs hiding under a rock? No! It's time to rise up and be counted, and stand upon Jesus the Rock. The church is at a tipping point. We're in danger, if Jesus tarries, of losing the fight. The gates of hell are working hard to destroy the church. Thankfully, Jesus said, *"Upon this rock I will build my church, and all the powers of hell will not conquer it"* (Matt. 16:18 NLT). This is a Biblical promise about Christ. In love I say, "To those who don't believe God's Word, you're fine to live how you please. Stop pulling out bite sized pieces to fit your program. Believe it all, or believe none of it." God demands a choice; search your heart today.

The time has come to wake up Luke-warm Christians and embrace all of God's inspired Word (1 Cor. 2:12-13). Luke-warm hearts struggle to accept the entire Bible as truth. They say they follow after Jesus, but won't obey His every Word. That is a problem with the Lord. Either the Bible is the inspired Word, or it isn't truth at all. To move from a Luke-warm Christian to a true follower of Jesus (category number one) takes a new way of thinking. There can be no doubt that all of it, every part, of the Bible comes from God (2 Tim. 3:16-17). Skeptics will always want to focus on the puzzling parts of the Bible. Think of it this way, the difficult areas are there to make us dig, search and study the

Good Book. The Amplified Bible says, *"Study and be eager and do your utmost to present yourself to God approved (tested by trial), a workman who has no cause to be ashamed, correctly analyzing and accurately dividing [rightly handling and skillfully teaching] the Word of Truth"* (2 Tim. 2:15). My prayer for this group is, "Lord, wake up the Luke-warm church before it is too late. Bring revival today."

Choice number three – YOU'RE DEAD

Zombies are a phenomenon in our culture. Movies and television shows like: *The Walking Dead, Night of the Living Dead, Warm Bodies, World War Z*, permeate our lives. The fascination with zombies; those mindless, flesh-eating, undead beings that wander around aimlessly, pursuing living flesh are growing. While Zombies are fictional creatures, spiritually speaking, they are real to life. Spiritual zombies are people without Christ. They go through the motions physically, but biblically they are spiritually dead. Ephesians 2:1-2 says, *"He made alive, who were dead in trespasses and sins, in which you once walked according to the course of this world, according to the prince of the power of the air, the spirit who now works in the sons of disobedience."* God loves spiritual zombies. He gives them opportunities to be turned to God and come to spiritual life. The Bible calls this *"Being Born again"* (John 3:3). Until a heart without Christ is made new (2 Cor. 5:17), these people are the true enemies of God (Rom. 5:10). Only God knows the motives of a man's heart. It is Jesus who draws the line concerning those who are on his team or not. In Matthew 12:30 He said, *"He who is not with Me is against Me, and he who does not gather with Me scatters abroad."*

Do you remember what it was like living without hope and peace? At one time all of us, in our hearts and minds, and because of sin, were once *"Alienated from God and were enemies"* (Colossians 1:21). It is sin that separates us from God

> A *Christian Zombie*
> *"Those who are spiritually comatose when it comes to the Word of God."*

(Rom. 3:23). It is sin that makes the living dead. I know it sounds harsh and uncaring to call people "dead spiritually." In reality, apart from a relationship with Jesus Christ, we are *"dead in our sins."* It is God who makes us alive through Christ (Colossians 2:13). The fact is; zombies are just people full of sin. Gandhi said, "Hate the sin, and love the sinner." We must never be ashamed to follow our biblical mandate. We should love lost people because lost people matter to God. Our job is to love the sinner all the way to Jesus. My prayer for this group is, "Lord, let your Holy Spirit draw in the lost. Make them alive in Christ and set them free from *"The law of sin and death"* (Rom. 8:2).

Chapter 3 – God is Gone

"Your iniquities have separated you from your
God; and your sins have hidden His face from
you, so that He will not hear" –Isaiah 59:2

The Christian Culture is changing

My concern is for the condition of the local church. Has God
hidden His face from the church in America? Some would disagree,
but the evidence is overwhelming, which I hope to bring to light
in this book. Somehow we have become distant from the God of
the Bible. It's as though we are in a season where our iniquities
have separated us from God. Has our sin caught up to us? Many
are crying out, while the multitudes sit back and contend that
everything is fine. Everything is not fine. As a Presbyter, Bill
Johnston, one of the pastors under my care recently wrote me,
"Hello, Please pray for me as I am getting a bit discouraged. We
have had special guests; we are worshipping and preaching our
hearts out. Property and sound systems have been upgraded.
Yet, the commitment level in our church remains at a low. Not sure
what to do. Seriously need your prayers." I assured him that he is
not alone. Like Bill, many pastors are perplexed by the condition
of the church. It's obvious; the Christian culture is different today.
I remember when nothing kept me from going to church. Not
so today, people are filled with excuses. The excuses are a dime

a dozen. Where did the passion and drive for the Lord go? It is evident by the lack of commitment in local churches. Even so-called strong Christians don't want to be discipled and get involved as in the past. People are resistant to sound Biblical teaching and doctrine. They walk away when corrected, rebuked, or asked to deal with sin. What many Christians really want is encouragement and to be unchallenged by their lifestyle choices. In 2 Timothy 3:16 it says, *"All Scripture is given by inspiration of God, and is profitable for doctrine, for reproof, for correction, for instruction in righteousness, that the man of God may be complete, thoroughly equipped for every good work."* Today, many Christians are being taught that everything can be hidden under the word "Grace." The phenomenon of using parts of scripture is occurring all across out great land. Overall, there is a deep sense that something is not right in the Christian culture. Things are changing, but not for the good. My hope is that God is watching and waiting to make His move. We need a Holy Ghost revival again.

I agreed with one of the old-time pastors in my city who said, "I've been around long enough to see the pendulum of the church swing both ways." Currently, it is swung wide left. One of the nation's Christian leaders, Rob Bell, in November 3, 2013 interviewed with Oprah Winfrey and stated, "There is a growing sense that when it comes to God, we're at the end of one era and the start of another, an entire mode of understanding and talking about God is dying as something new is being birthed." Like Ananias the Chief priest who prophesied that Jesus would die for the whole nation of Israel (John 11:49-52), Mr. Bell is prophesying, without knowing it, over the state of Christianity today.

Those paying attention should be very apprehensive about this changing conversation Bell speaks of. The emerging church and the seeker-friendly mentality focus on God's love, grace and forgiveness. These are vital subjects of scripture and must be taught. The rising persuasion is to shy away from the harder truths in scripture. The conversation has shifted. These pastor's and leaders don't categorically preach on sin, hell and judgment with conviction. I know pastors, priests and others who have said to my face, "I don't preach on those topics." At a local ministers meeting one man absolutely said, "I don't preach on anything accept love and forgiveness." I stood there trying to reconcile his words. I think I was in shock.

Preaching the lighter side of the gospel is trending upwards, while the prevailing wind in Christian culture is to practically ignore the hard truths. Overall, the people are getting a soft, watered-down gospel. This growing fad has taken our local churches and Christians culture hostage. There is a new spirit in town.

For a season God is allowing this apathetic, lazy, and sin filled culture to rise up. Sermon titles like, *"Eight steps to having a wonderful life"* bleed from American pulpits. We don't dare change the title to: *"Eight ways to stop living in sin...then you can have a wonderful life."* Author John MacArthur in an interview for *Grace to You,* said "What we have today floating out there in the market-minded, church-growth movement is a synthetic gospel. It's a fabrication of marketing guys, people who are trying to find what sells. And it's not the true gospel! I'm not offering a new gospel. What I'm doing is taking people back to the only gospel that exists, and bringing that gospel to bear against what is essentially a new gospel being offered today." When the Word of God has become passé, watch out, judgment is coming.

A Fundamental Shift

Where are the crosses, alters, biblical doctrine, and alter calls? Their growing absence is a telling sign that the local church is distancing itself from the past. Change is one thing, but fundamental change is dangerous. The American Heritage Dictionary defines the word fundamental as, "Something that is an essential or necessary part of a system or object." There is a fundamental shift happening in our churches. The conversations are changing and the biblical model is being replaced. The Word of God is slowly being supplanted with false teaching and doctrines of demons, which the Holy Spirit warned would come in the last days (1 Tim. 4:1-3).

This change in our essentials is a movement away from God's plan. Our lack of understanding has caught the church off guard. Our failure to deal with it has spread to our nation. In 2008, just

> "The cross is to Christians as Mickey Mouse is to Disney"

before he won the presidency, Barack Obama boldly proclaimed, "We are five days away from fundamentally transforming the United States of America." This is happening before our very eyes. We are becoming a nation dependent upon the government to provide nearly everything. When the masses continually look to the government as their source, instead of God, judgment is coming. In the church, many prominent leaders are trying to fundamentally change the gospel and the way the local church operates. This shift that Bell speaks of is a subtle moving away from our Biblical roots. Globes and other modern designs adorn church sanctuaries and the cross has all but been eliminated. In 1 Corinthians 1:18 it declares, *"For the message of the cross is foolishness to those who are perishing, but to us who are being saved it is the power of God."* Think about it, if the cross is the power of God for new believers, why take it out of the local church? After all, if the target of the seeker and emerging church is *"those who are being saved"* shouldn't the cross be everywhere. It doesn't make any sense. J. Vernon McGee says, "The cross divides men. The cross divides the saved from the unsaved, but it doesn't divide the saved people. It should unite them." The cross is to Christians, as Mickey Mouse is to Disney. Or, imagine Hershey's without chocolate? The cross is central to the gospel. We expect believers to *"Take up their cross daily"* (Luke 9:23), but won't let one be seen on Sunday. This sends a conflicting message to those we want to reach. For a pastor or preacher to stand in the pulpit and preach on the cross, then have to defend its absence in the very building is a conflict of interest. Maybe this is why many preachers don't preach on the cross. How can preachers NOT preach on the cross? If a church doesn't preach all-the-gospel, is it considered to be a Bible believing church? Have we, in our ignorance, opened the door to this kind of foolish thinking in our nation? In July of 2010 the White House demanded that the cross of Jesus Christ be covered up when President Obama spoke at Georgetown Catholic University. By the way, Catholics schools are identified by the cross. Maybe our nation is reaping what the Christian community has been sowing?

The Real Seeker

The whole concept of the seeker-friendly church is perplexing. In Romans 3:11 the Apostle Paul tells us, *"There is no one who understands, no one who seeks God."* The concept of unbelievers being *"God-seekers"* is unbiblical. Think about it, what unbeliever that you know seeks after God? For the most part, they don't want anything to do with the local church, the Bible and especially God. However, it is biblical that the Father is the real seeker. John 6:44 settles the case, *"No one can come to Me unless the Father who sent Me draws him."* It's clear that nobody gets saved unless the Father searches him out. Besides, it is because of unrighteousness that *"The wrath of God is revealed"* (Romans 1:18), which many seeker-sensitive pastors refuse to preach about. Sadly, the church is playing right into the hands of the enemy. Every time we fail to challenge the people with the hard-truths of the gospel, we weaken the Body of Christ. If we continue down this path more of God's people *"Will not endure sound doctrine, but according to their own desires, because they have itching ears, they will heap up for themselves teachers; and they will turn their ears away from the truth, and be turned aside to fables"* (2 Tim. 4:3-4).

Sermons filled with the fluffy, soft, and non-threatening fragments of the gospel, is only doing the seeker a disservice. The large churches and swelling crowds in the "seeker sensitive" model is a ruse. While they produced numerical growth, overall they do not produce spiritual growth. How do we know this? There is a telling quote by one of the founders of the seeker sensitive movement, in an article by Dwight A. Randall. The article is entitled "Bill Hybells' *frank admission about "seeker friendly" churches.* The quote reads, "Hybels, who is to be commended for his frankness, adds, 'We made a mistake. What we should have done when people crossed the line of faith and became Christians, we should have started telling people and teaching people that they have to take responsibility to become 'self feeders.' We should have gotten people, taught people, how to read their bible between services, how to do the spiritual practices much more aggressively on their own.'"

Is this seeker-friendly model going to work? The fact is; *"For if this plan or this work is of men, it will come to nothing; but if it is of God, you cannot overthrow it--lest you even be found to fight against God."* (Acts 5:38-39). The dust is settling on this flawed philosophy. Time is revealing the truth. Erroneous teaching and doctrine will not last. There is a vast contrast when comparing the basic philosophy of the seeker-friendly sensitive church to Jesus' ministry. In Matthew 10:34 Jesus said, *"I did not come to bring peace but a sword."* Matthew Henry's Commentary says, "Christ came to give the sword of the Word, with which his disciples fight against the world, and conquering work this sword has made." Rob Bell is right, the conversation has turned. The focus has become *"peace"* (finding common ground with the world). Therefore the sword, which is the Word of God (which is Christ), is being used to stab our own message in the back. *"There is nothing new under the sun"* (Eccl. 1:9). It is time we got back to the New Testament model.

The Bigger Barns Mentality

In Luke 12:16-21 Jesus tells *The Parable of the Rich Fool*. While the obvious meaning of this parable is greed, it also deals with the symptoms of greed. The Intervarsity Press (IVP) New Testament Commentary Series calls this disease, "Possessionitis." The commentary goes on to say "Jesus attacks this disease directly in this parable because it appears that greed and the pursuit of possessions constitute one of the greatest obstacles to spiritual growth." While this is especially true in our technologically savvy world and modern culture, I see another issue. A spirit, a mentality, has become attached to the farmer. He has become blind to the future. This same blindness affects many believers today. I call it the "Bigger Barn Mentality." Here's is the parable of the rich fool:

> Then He spoke a parable to them, saying: "The ground of a certain rich man yielded plentifully. And he thought within himself, saying, 'What shall I do, since I have no room to store my crops?' So he said, 'I will do this: I will pull down my barns and build greater, and there I will store all my crops and my goods. And I will say to my soul, "Soul, you have many goods laid up for many years; take your ease; eat, drink, and be merry."' But God said to him, 'Fool! This night your soul will be required of you; then whose will those things be which you have provided?' "So is he who lays up treasure for himself, and is not rich toward God." -Luke 12:16-21

The farmer was a happy man. He was rich and had a good harvest. Something was missing; he wasn't rich toward God. In verse 19 of the New Living Testament (NLT) he said, "I'll sit back and say to myself, "My friend, you have enough stored away for years to come. Now take it easy! Eat, drink, and be merry!'"

In one sense, building bigger barns meant security, but he is neglecting the other side of the coin. While he focused on the now, he wasn't thinking about what was to come. This man reminds me of this seeker-friendly culture. Generally speaking, seeker-friendly pastors, refuse to warn the people about sin, falling away, deception and judgment. Amazingly, all of these things are here now. Living under "Grace" doesn't mean we can lower God's standard of living. Jude 1:4 warns about *"Certain men have crept in unnoticed, who long ago were marked out for this condemnation, ungodly men, who turn the grace of our God into lewdness and deny the only Lord God and our Lord Jesus Christ."* J. Gresham Machen said, "The very center and core of the whole Bible is the doctrine of the grace of God." The Bigger Barn Mentality uses grace to harbor the sin and hidden wickedness inside our hearts. A study of the word grace will reveal that grace isn't a license to sin, but a call to repentance and right-living. Maybe then, we'll put down our beers and pick up the Word. If the grace of God continues to become lewdness, we're doing down fast. *"When the foundation be destroyed, what can the righteous do?"* (Psalm 11:3).

The seeker sensitive movement and the shifting Christian culture may be in vogue. Its leaders are riding this wave of extreme popularity for now; possibly poised to become the next mega-church. They may have all the tools, everything needed to bring in the lost. Yet, like Willow Creek, in the long run they will come to realize their flocks are undernourished and spiritually impoverished. When seekers are told little about sin, hell and judgment, they're getting only part of the gospel. It's like giving a thirsty and starving man only water. He can survive for a while longer, but eventually he will starve to death. Christians cannot survive on milk alone (1 Cor. 3:2). Let's be truthful, if Jesus

> *Many local churches have everything they need to win the LOST. Sadly, they don't do it.*

29

preached on hell, separation from God, sin, and the judgment to come, shouldn't we? The seeker mentality argues that reducing Bible readings to a verse or two is perfectly okay. That preaching should focus on the "felt needs" of seekers. They say, "Don't be hard on them; they might not come back to church." Instead, entertain them and keep the Biblical content light; which is vital to their cause.

The farmer loved success and wanted more. So, he tore down his existing barns to build bigger and better ones. He wasn't content with what he had. This is like the way the world is accepting of the seeker-friendly mega-church environment. Why does the world have room for this mentality? S. Michael Houdman says, "The focus of the seeker church is not Christ-centered, but man-centered." Let me compare this to the Word of God. The farmer didn't like his original barns. Hidden inside his heart dwelt the spirits of fear, worldliness, selfishness and greed. He wanted more of the wrong things. The Word of God is like the barns. Everything we need to know is inside the barns God has given. His Word is enough. Today, we are dismantling it for something new. We don't need bigger barns; we need to know what is inside the existing ones.

The seeker mentality demands little from the people, which is opposite the Bible. Unlike the farmer, we must get back to being *"Rich toward God"* (Luke 12:21), leaving worldly thinking behind. Like the farmer our culture has become greedy for new barns and worldly philosophies. The Bible isn't relevant enough anymore. It's been reduced to another book in a Christian's library. The Mormon religion promotes "Another Testament of Jesus Christ." To them, and many in our Christian culture, the Bible is just a piece of their puzzle. Do these people truly believe Jesus and

His Word? Today the Wycliffe Bible Translators and their allies have produced a Muslim friendly Bible. According to Yahoo News "Christians concerned about the translations have failed to persuade these agencies to retain 'Father' and 'Son' in the text of all their translations." The Yahoo article goes on to describe another group Frontiers "Who produced *Meaning of the Gospel of Christ*, an Arabic translation which removes 'Father' in reference to God and replaces it with 'Allah,' and removes or redefines 'Son.'" These actions should not only raise an eyebrow or two, but should cause us to expect God's judgment to fall. Here is an example of how Matthew 28:19 is changed.

- **The Bible says**, *"Go therefore and make disciples of all the nations, baptizing them in the name of the Father and of the Son and of the Holy Spirit."*
- **The Arabic translation says**, *"Cleanse them by water in the name of Allah, his Messiah and his Holy Spirit."*

Reaching so-called seekers, Muslims or anyone for that matter is a worthy calling. At the same time, to alter, leave out parts, or reject the Word of God is wrong to the core. Changing who Jesus is, or what He said is the greatest tragedy of all. To treat God's Word as imperfect when He says, *"His way is perfect; The word of the Lord is proven"* (Psalm 18:30) is a major problem. To treat God's word with contempt is to call Him a liar. Surly, God will intervene when His Word; doctrines, pages and verses are conveniently ignored. Our willingness to skip over key passages to fit our model of ministry is a mentality that will come at a high cost. To accept mere parts of the Bible; not all of it puts it on the same level as any other book.

This is detrimental because people aren't hearing the full truth. This means that God's people; especially new converts and seekers, don't fully understand that *"If anyone comes to Me (Jesus) and does not hate his father and mother, wife and children, brothers and sisters, yes, and his own life also, he cannot be My (Jesus') disciple"* (Luke 14:26). The Common English Version says, *"You cannot be my disciple, unless you love me more than you love your father and mother, your wife and children, and your brothers and sisters. You cannot come with me unless you love me more than you love your own life."*

What is the whole council of God? The Apostle Paul knew, *"Therefore I testify to you this day that I am innocent of the blood of all men. For I have not shunned to declare to you the whole counsel of God"* (Acts 20:26-27). It is God's revelation of His Son Jesus Christ. Paul did not suppress any truths, and never compromised the good news. Matthew Henry's Commentary says, "This counsel of God it is the business of ministers to declare as it is revealed, and not otherwise nor any further." Yet, somewhere along the way it has been compromised. Today, the message has become lopsided. The New Living Translation says it like this, *"I declare today that I have been faithful. If anyone suffers eternal death, it's not my fault, for I didn't shrink from declaring all that God wants you to know."* In his sermon (# 2233) Charles Spurgeon says, "Most truths have two sides, and it is well to try to see both of them. Nearly every doctrine in the Word of God is balanced by some other doctrine, and many of the differences amongst the people of God have arisen from undue stress which has been laid on one aspect of truth, while the other side has been altogether neglected. This danger very frequently besets us." Maybe one day, the scales used to weigh Biblical teaching and preaching is going to be revealed. Which doctrines and principals will outweigh the others? Which pulpits lack balance? Like Paul, will we be innocent of the blood of all men?

In the parable, God calls the farmer a fool. Biblically, a fool is at the bottom of God's pecking order. The Psalmist paints the picture for the Lord. *"The fool has said in his heart 'there is no God'"* (Ps. 14:1). Like an atheist or an unbeliever the farmer was a fool. He couldn't see the broader scope. The bigger picture didn't enter his mind. Like the farmer, people are being taught to forget about judgment, sin, hell and destruction. This is a part of God's bigger picture for us. Eternity, heaven and everlasting life are the omega, and come at the end. We have become too motivated about "here" (earth), and fail to focus on "there" (eternity). God's Word shows us how to live on earth and not love it. We are to be pilgrims, not God settlers. God doesn't want bigger barns. God wants us to die to self, not live for self. As a Christian culture we have placed most of our eggs in the wrong basket. For the most part, the church has been deceiving the flock. This must end. As the farmer failed to realize, *"Today his soul will be required of him"* (vs. 20), people need to fully understand that judgment is coming. The Bible hasn't changed; God will require this of us also. That goes for ministers who preach and people who hear. The Amplified Bible says, *"This very night they [the messengers of God] will demand your soul of you."* The Common English Version says it like this, *"Fool, tonight you will die."*

God will not tolerate evil for long

Many people today have forgotten that God *"Disciplines those He loves"* (Heb. 12:6). This is not just a New Testament concept (see Prov. 3:12). How long will God allow a preacher immersed in sin to continue to shine? How many warnings and opportunities to repent does our *"Long-suffering"* Lord give? Oh, be sure, the hammer will fall. As God's children we must *"Endure divine discipline"* (Heb. 12:7-13). As preachers, we nullify many scriptures when we don't educate people on how and why God corrects us.

One writer said, "Discipline is how God lovingly turns His children from rebellion to obedience." In this soft spiritual climate, we have succeeded in taking the spotlight off of the harshness of discipline, judgment and hell. But, this is merely placating to people's fears, and not conveying a clear picture of Almighty God. What happens when God disciplines a person who only knows of His love and forgiveness? They will understand God via man's wisdom, and not from scripture.

One thing that will never change; God does not tolerate evil for very long. He will eventually deal with it in His own way and in His perfect timing. One thing that has changed though is that the Body of Christ (believers) has begun to tolerate evil. Evil has everything to do with the heart. As the heart of man continues to wink at sin, our culture will continue to slide deeper in the abyss of evil. Evil is having its season. An evil heart sums up the life of ancient King Rehoboam. Being a descendant of King Solomon, the wisest man to ever live meant little to this king. He had the advantage of a good family, the education only a prince could have, money and possessions, and even strong leadership, yet he still blew it big time. The Bible calls him "evil." Why was Rehoboam evil? The same reason people are today. 2 Chronicles 12:2 (NIV) says, *"He did evil because he had not set his heart on seeking the Lord."*

God always deals with evil one way or another. Clearly, *"It is God who judges"* (Psalm 75:7). The fact that many preachers and religious organizations refuse to take evil and judgment seriously is a mind-bender. One day soon the judge is going to punish sin, wickedness, and evil. It's not a matter of if, but when the fires of judgment sweep through hearts and churches. Soon, judgment will hit the shores of our nation too. America is the greatest nation in history, but she has sinned. America has fallen short because the Body of Christ (His church) has taken its eyes off of God. Seeker sensitive congregations beware, *"Judgment begins at the house of God"* (1 Peter 4:7). In fact, all churches, pastors, leaders and people within the house of the Lord will face God. Unfortunately, like the church of Ephesus, America has *"Left her first love"* (Rev 2:4).

The following is from a letter by Billy Graham posted on the Billy Graham Evangelistic Association website: *"Some years ago, my wife, Ruth, was reading the draft of a book I was writing. When she finished a section describing the terrible downward spiral of our nation's moral standards and the idolatry of worshiping false gods such as technology and sex, she startled me by exclaiming, 'If God doesn't punish America, He'll have to apologize to Sodom and Gomorrah'"* (see Genesis 19). That is a pretty serious statement. By the way, in Ezekiel 16:49-50 God explains why he destroyed those two cities. *"Look, this was the iniquity of your sister Sodom: She and her daughter had pride, fullness of food, and abundance of idleness; neither did she strengthen the hand of the poor and needy. And they were haughty and committed abomination before Me; therefore I took them away as I saw fit."* I'm curious; would this message ever be spoken inside one of our seeker-friendly or politically correct churches today? Make no mistake about it, and don't be deceived, judgment is coming to the church, America, and the world. Things are going to get really ugly; just read the book of Revelation. Sin is no joking matter to God. Maybe there is a coming revival that will change everything. I hope so.

True followers of Jesus

Revival will wake up the sleeping church. Revival will produce true followers of Jesus. John was a true follower of Jesus. The things that were revealed to John on the island of Patmos produced the Revelation of Jesus Christ, the last book of the Bible. John witnessed the end, the final judgment of God on the church, mankind and Satan. Revelation, the final book of the New Testament and its judgments are looming. Never before could we say with as much certainty, Jesus is *"At the door"* (Rev. 3:20). We are at the beginning of the end. Further proof is the *"Spirit of Antichrist, which you have heard is coming, and is now already in the world"* (1 John 4:3). This lying and deceiving spirit is already bombarding our faith and eroding our Biblical foundation. In the eyes of many, America is no longer considered a Christian nation. The lies and deception can be seen from the White House, to the courthouse. Evil and compromise has crept in from the house on the street into the church house. People, calling themselves Christians, sit in the pews, but don't actually follow Jesus. This error has flooded the streets of America and even greater, the local church.

Jesus had many disciples, true followers. In Antioch the disciples were first labeled Christians (Acts 11:26). They walked, followed and died for Him. In John 8:31 Jesus was speaking to those who believed Him, *"If you abide in My word, you are My disciples indeed."* People like Joseph of Arimathea became a disciple of Jesus (Matt. 27:57). The New American Standard Bible (NASB) Topical Bible says, "A disciple is a 'learner,' 'follower,' or 'adherent' of a particular leader." Throughout the church age, people were known as disciples of Jesus. As we move to the end of the church age, things are changing. In America we rarely use the term "Disciple." Jesus said, *"Whoever wants to be my disciple must deny themselves and take up their cross and follow me"* (Matt. 16:24). Disciple is used 27 times in the New Testament to describe the followers of Jesus. There are 3 requirements or musts to become a disciple, a true follower, and a Christian; and there are 9 disqualifications:

Whoever wants to be a disciple...MUST BE

- **Denying self** – Death to self is not optional for believers. *"I tell you the truth, unless a kernel of wheat falls to the ground and dies, it remains only a single seed. But if it dies, it produces many seeds. The man who loves his life will lose it, while the man who hates his life in this world will keep it for eternal life"* (John 12:24 NIV). We must stop saying, "I am a Christian" if we're not willing to check ourselves at the door.

- **Bearing the cross** – The cross means suffering and death. As true followers of Christ *"Count it all joy when you fall into various trials"* (James 1:2). We must stop saying, "I am a Christian" if we're not willing to pick up our pain, suffering and trials, with the right attitude.

- **Following after Jesus** – True followers walk as Jesus walked. They are always being about the Fathers business. This is a daily commitment that never bends or compromises; "values, lifestyle, economics and politics with the predominate culture of society" (Kurt Stuckmeyer). We must stop saying, "I am a Christian" if we're not willing to follow Jesus' Word, the Bible without excuses. Jesus made it clear that we either follow Him or we don't.

9 ways to be disqualified as a disciple of Christ
- **Failing to serve those in authority** (Matt. 10:24-25).
- **Putting others before Christ** (Luke 14:26).
- **Unwilling to suffering and die for Christ daily** (Luke 14:27).
- **Putting things before Christ** (Luke 14:33).
- **Failing to deny one's self** (Matt. 16:24).
- **Failing to walk like Jesus walked** (Matt. 16:24).
- **Neglecting the Word of God** (John 8:31).

- **Failing to love one another** (John 13:35).
- **Bearing little or no fruit** (John 15:8).

Taking back the meaning of "Christian"

The use of the word Christian has been hijacked. Has it been stolen from you? It is high time we take responsibility for the name we use. To call oneself a Christian and not live up to the three standards Jesus established is in error. While nobody is perfect, we all fall short of Jesus' high standard. No true follower wants to be disqualified. There are many more "Christians in name only" (CINO) out there then we realize. *"Millions of people throughout the world call themselves Christians. From Roman Catholics to Protestants, from fundamentalists to liberals, there are many different perspectives about what it means to be a Christian. One can become lost in the complexity of belies, dogmas, moral injunctions, and religious rites. But the larger context–that of a daily life–it is often impossible to distinguish one Christian from another, or even a Christian from a non-Christian"* (followingJesus.org). We must do much better as believers.

Jesus demanded that His followers live exactly as He commanded. Its over 2,000 years later, where is the permission to live different. The Bible hasn't changed, we have. In John 8:31-32 Jesus looked at those Jews who believed in Him and said,

> *The word "Christian" has been hijacked. It doesn't mean what it once meant.*

"If you abide in My word, you are my disciples. And you shall know the truth, and the truth shall make you free." These words ring throughout the corridors of time to each one of us. The word *"Abide"* means: to accept or act in accordance with a rule, decision, or recommendation. The synonyms for the world *"Abide"* are:

39

comply with, obey, observe, follow, keep to, adhere to, stick to, stand by, act in accordance with, uphold, heed, accept, go along with, acknowledge, respect, etc.

Today, some believers no-longer follow the teachings of Jesus. Jesus is the Word. To stop following Him, is to stop following the Bible. This means the Bible has become just another book to them. Does our lack of love and devotion for Jesus' Word prove our lack of love for Jesus Himself? Everything in me says yes. Does our unwillingness to preach or hear the "whole gospel" mean we have forgotten why we're here on earth in the first place. Yes, a resounding yes. One look at current church statistics makes the disturbing case that believers today are losing the battle. Simply pointing to; church attendance, loving one another, forgiving one another, tithing, and most other basic gospel principles confirms we are not abiding with Christ and His Word. The local church is losing the battle because people, who we're once dedicated, are no longer committed. People don't wake up on Sunday morning and say, "I'm quitting God." The thing that leaves church leader's scratching their heads is a phenomenon I call, "Apostasy Attenders." We don't really notice when a person goes from becoming a four-times a month attender to a three-times a month attender. Eventually, the disappearing act continues; they become two-time a month attender. Then before you know it, the pastor is saying, "Where are George and his family?"

This phenomenon is another sign of the End-times and has many of our local churches struggling to survive. They don't have the crowds or the resources to make a dent in their communities. I have witnessed this first hand. There are many seeker-sensitive churches that have the people, but not the biblical drive. They have larger crowds, but small passion to warn the people about what is coming. In my own small town, I have seen this. A Holy Ghost revival is the only thing that will wake up the church. We need a lasting season of God's fire.

Thank God, Jesus is coming back soon

When the people who know the least, know it the loudest, God will come again. I'm just glad Jesus is coming back. He's coming again because He wants to be with us (John 14:1-4). The desire for a relationship with us is a passion of the Father. In John 15:4 Jesus reminds us of His desire for connection with us. He says, *"Abide in Me, and I in you. As the branch cannot bear fruit of itself, unless it abides in the vine, neither can you, unless you abide in Me."* Thankfully, like Noah and Lot, God is coming to rescue and save the End-time church (1 Thess. 1:10). He is coming for those who have kept His commands and His Word to endure. Therefore He says, *"I also will keep you from the hour of trial which shall come upon the whole world, to test those who dwell on the earth"* (Rev. 3:10). I believe Jesus is coming back soon. Here are several reasons why I believe this:

- Evil continues to out-distance good, God will come again.
- Christians have become more like the world, instead of the reverse, God will come again.
- "We fear men so much because we fear God so little" (William Gurnall), God will come again.
- The Christian culture bends over backward to appease so-called seekers of God, rather than strive to please our Heavenly Father, God will come again.
- Sunday morning consists of sleeping homes, quiet streets and empty churches, God will come again.

- We continually misquote, misinterpret and misrepresent God's Holy Book, God will come again.
- Christian's in name only (CINO people) continue to be the voice representing Christ to the world, God will come again.
- God's standards become so low, that Moody Bible Institute, and several other Christian organizations, universities and colleges drop their ban on alcohol, and tobacco use for their facilities and staff, God will come again.
- Leaders; national, local and church continue to thumb their noses at *"Doing what is right"* (1 Thess. 3:13), God will come again.
- The Christian community fails to do the work of the Lord, because they *"Profess to know God, but in works deny Him"* (Titus 1:16), God will come again.
- Leaders; religious and political draw near to God with their mouths, and honor God with their lips, but in reality, their hearts are far from Him (Matt. 15:8), God will come again.
- So-called Christian denominations, many of who are *"Wolves in sheep's clothing"* (Matt. 7:15) continue leading God's sheep astray, God will come again.
- We continue to worship and serve created things instead of God, we repeatedly *"Exchange the truth of God for a lie"* (Rom. 1:25), God will come again.
- We stop adhering to Biblical doctrine to appease the politically correct society, God will come again.

Did John the Revelator, in one of his many visions see the apostate church? He knew about the growing evil in his time. Maybe that's why, in Revelation 22:20 he said, *"Come quickly"*

Lord Jesus. The Apostle Paul continually warned that Christ *"May establish your heart blameless before God and Father, at the coming of our Lord Jesus with all his saints"* (1 Thess. 3:13). Both John and Paul were echoing Jesus' comments in John 14:3, *"I will come again"* and *"Surely I am coming quickly"* (Rev. 22:20). Both were undoubtedly aware of Satan's power, lies and plans to destroy the church.

Several months ago I was reading when Jesus was facing the cross; the Lord showed me something interesting. The same players, killing and destroying the literal body of Christ, at the end of the age of the law (Moses to Jesus), are the same players today at the end of the age of grace (the church age). They are the same people hurting and killing the Body of Christ (His church) today. If we are really at the end of this age, Jesus is coming soon. He is coming to not only spare the righteous from the wrath to come, but to *"Judge the living and the dead"* (1 Peter 4:5). Judgment is next on the prophetic clock. Jesus said, *"Behold, I am coming soon! My reward is with me, and I will give to everyone according to what he has done"* (Rev. 22:12).

The play is almost over

The Apostle Peter points to something every local church should be emphasizing. He says, *"The end of all things is at hand; therefore be serious and watchful in your prayers"* (1 Peter 4:7). C.S. Lewis warned, *"God will invade. But I wonder whether people who ask God to interfere openly and directly in our world quite realize what it will be like when He does. When that happens, it is the end of the World. When the author walks on the stage the play is over."*

As a pastor during this season of apostasy, it breaks my heart to witness the continued weakening of our faith. Too many believe that everything is okay, but it isn't. Before the play comes to a close, I believe God is going to visit us again. Like in the upper room, He will pour out his spirit (see Acts 2). I'm saddened and excited at the same time. Regardless of many in the church who are MIA (missing in action), The Father has placed a great anticipation for revival in me and many others. I'm hoping, doing, believing, praying, and waiting for a Holy Ghost revival to come. As our nation rapidly descends into the Marianas Trench of evil, we must fight until the trumpet sounds (1 Cor. 15:52). The deeper and deeper we fall, the more we pray *"Will You not revive us again, that Your people may rejoice in You?"* (Psalm 85:6). The more we sledgehammer to chip away our foundation, which are the Biblical principles we were founded upon, the more we cry out, *"Restore us, O LORD God of hosts; cause Your face to shine, and we shall be saved!"* (Psalm 80:19). As we watch sin, the culprit of our condition, plunge us into a "spiritual dark ages" we must be strong until our eyes *"Have seen the King, the Lord of hosts"* (Isaiah 6:5). While we try and thrive with the people God has given us, we cannot lose sight of *"The latter rain"* (Joel 2:23) God promised to bring upon us. Lord Jesus, come quickly.

The stolen seed

We live in a time when we have forgotten what our Heavenly Father promised. Jesus said, *"Let not your heart be troubled; you believe in God, believe also in Me. In My Father's house are many mansions; if it were not so, I would have told you. I go to prepare a place for you. And if I go and prepare a place for you, I will come again and receive you to Myself; that where I am, there you may be also"* (John 14:1-3). Not only have we forgotten what Jesus said to the church, but also what He said to each of us. Jesus has wonderful promises pertaining to life and how to live it strong. He says, *"Grace and peace be multiplied to you in the knowledge of God and of Jesus our Lord, as His divine power has given to us all things that pertain to life and godliness, through the knowledge of Him who called us by glory and virtue, by which have been given to us exceedingly great and precious promises, that through these you may be partakers of the divine nature, having escaped the corruption that is in the world through lust"* (2 Peter 2:1-4). What are the precious promises of God in your life? Do you remember them? They are there, like a seed planted long ago, waiting to shoot forth.

God often speaks through the gift of prophecy. Someone has the *"Word of the Lord"* (Acts 16:32; Ezekiel 13:2) for you. In the last days God said, *"And it shall come to pass afterward that I will pour out My Spirit on all flesh; your sons and your daughters shall prophesy, your old men shall see visions. And also on My men-servants and on My maid-servants I will pour out My Spirit in those days"* (Joel 2:28-29). Many including myself have had the privilege to receive God's promises by dreams and visions. I joke telling people, I'm stuck in the middle. I'm not an old man, or a young man, so I get both dreams and visions. Mostly, the promises come from reading and studying the Word of God. Unfortunately many of us have lost the power and strength of the Lord. We worry, stress, and lack faith over life's struggles and trials. In the Parable of the Sower (Matthew 13), some of the seed, which is the Word of God, fell among thorns. Jesus explained, *"Now he who receives seed among thorns is he who hears the word, and the cares of this world and the deceitfulness of riches choke the word, and he becomes unfruitful"* (Matt. 13:22). I'm tired of watching the enemy steal the seed of God's Word from our hearts. He does this to local churches and ministries as well. In a sermon called, *Taking Back what has been stolen from You,* Benny Hinn says *"True riches are coming to the Body of Christ, and you can trigger the outpouring in your own life by planting seed."* While he is referring to money as the seed, I want to keep the focus on the Word of God as the seed. Here is Rev. Hinn's quote again in bold letters and my commentary which follows:

- **True riches are coming** – This is not speaking of material things, which the bible calls "uncertain riches" warning us not to trust them (1 Tim. 6:17). True riches are *"To know the Love of Christ, which passes knowledge; that you may be filled with all the fullness of God"* (Eph. 3:19). To attain true riches one must have a relationship with Christ and an intimate knowledge of God, which comes from His Word.
- **To the Body of Christ** – The apostle Paul sums up who the body of Christ is. Speaking to the church in Corinth, he confirms *"Now you are the body of Christ, and members individually"* (1 Cor. 12:27). Then speaking to the church in Colossae about Jesus he adds, *"He is the head of the body, the church"* (Colossians 1:18). So, local churches are the body of Christ, and Jesus is the head of each church.
- **You can trigger the outpouring in your own life** – As the Holy Spirit was poured out on the Day of Pentecost, fire fell upon *"Each of them"* (Acts 2:3). Revival comes to the masses via the individuals within the masses. To trigger revival in you, get into the Word of God. The Word is the foundation of Revival. Psalm 119:154 says, *"Plead my cause and redeem me; revive me according to your word."*

- **By planting seed** – *"The seed is the Word of God"* (Luke 8:11). As a preacher of the Word the Apostle Paul said, *"I have planted"* (1 Cor. 3:6). When we plant the seed of God in us, something powerful grows. We can experience, the true riches of Christ, freedom in the body of Christ and genuine revival. When individuals can say to God, *"Your word I have hidden in my heart"* (Psalm 119:11), then sin will lose its grip. Then, the thorns of life will propel you from an unfruitful worker to one that is *"Fruitful and multiplies"* (Gen. 1:28). With the seed in place, a believer can walk *"worthy of the Lord, fully pleasing Him, being fruitful in every good work and increasing in the knowledge of God"* (Col. 1:10).

Losing the seed

For the Christian, life is ALL-ABOUT the seed, the Word of God. When someone loses their God-given seed, in this world it's hard to watch. No seed equals no blessing and no reaping. However, to see a precious brother or sister in Christ suffer because they didn't realize the seed was even gone in the first place is tragic and painful to watch. Every day good people in the body of Christ struggle because the seed, the Word, the gift, and the power to live for Christ seem to have disappeared. They struggle to *"Fight the good fight of the faith"* (1 Tim. 6:12). In the New King James, under 1 Timothy 4 is the heading, *"The Great Apostasy."* We learned in an earlier chapter this is referring to a period of time in the last days. I would like to compare those who's seed has been stolen to those who are mentioned as victims of the *"Great Apostasy"* also known as *"The falling away of the church."* Here is what 1 Timothy 4:1-3 declares, *"Now the Spirit expressly says that in latter times some will depart from the faith, giving heed to deceiving spirits and doctrine of demons, speaking lies in hypocrisy, having their own conscience seared."* For some reason, somewhere along the way, these people laid down their guard and the enemy came charging in to rob them blind. Here are a few biblical examples of those who didn't realize the power and promises of God had left them:

- **The people of Noah's time,** who were unaware that judgment was coming that very day. Noah preached that the rains and waters of judgment were coming, but they didn't believe him. They didn't realize judgment was near (Matt. 24:39). Today many live unaware, therefore we should *"Be ready, for the Son of Man is coming at an hour you do not expect"* (Matthew 24:44).

- **Hophni and Phinehas,** the two sons of Eli the priest, were evil. The Bible says, *"They did not know the Lord"* (1 Sam. 2:12). Despite countless warnings regarding their corrupt ways, they didn't realize, *"The Lord desired to kill them."* Today, many live their lives unaware that they desperately need Jesus. Be sure, God won't tolerate sin for long and will put an end to it. *"If man sins against another, God will judge him. But if a man sins against the Lord, who will intercede for him?"* (1 Sam. 2:25).

- **Samson,** who was a judge in Israel, lost the power God gave to him. When Delilah finally cut his hair and the Philistines came rushing in, He didn't realize his strength was gone. In the saddest Bible verse ever, *"He did not know that the LORD had departed from him"* (Judges 16:20). Many live their lives *"Having a form of godliness, but denying its power"* (2 Tim. 3:5).

- **King Saul**, Israel's first king, lost the most important thing. One day, *"The Spirit of the Lord departed from Saul, and a distressing spirit from the Lord troubled him"* (1 Sam. 16:14). Today, many don't realize that what they once had in God is gone. One day Jesus will respond, *"Not everyone who says to Me, 'Lord, Lord,' shall enter the kingdom of heaven, but he who does the will of My Father in heaven"* (Matt. 7:21).

- **Judas**, one of the chosen twelve disciples, ended up betraying the Lord. His motives are unclear. Was he pushing Jesus into establishing an earthly kingdom? Was he just a selfish, greedy guy trying to get ahead? Today, many don't realize that their good efforts are actually betraying the Son of God. Matthew 26:24 says, *"Woe to that man by whom the Son of Man is betrayed! It would have been good for that man if he had not been born."*

- **Luke-warm Christians**, those with the awesome privilege to live in the time before the return of Jesus Christ. They take the Word of God and compromise it away like, *"Throwing pearls before swine"* (Matt. 7:6). They don't realize they have *"Forgotten their first love"* (Rev. 2:4), and that God has provided for them everything needed *"For a godly life through our knowledge of him who called us by his own glory and goodness."* (2 Peter 1:3). They have everything needed to thrive for Christ, but chose to live in spiritual poverty. Therefore, God says, *"I will vomit you out of My mouth"* (Rev. 3:16).

Chapter 4 – 2 Gates, 2 Roads

*"Change your mind and change your whole
life experience"* —C.G. Rousing

Gates

We all go through gates. No, I'm not talking about Bill Gates the founder of Microsoft, although, if you own a computer, you have undoubtedly helped make Bill Gates one of the richest men in the world. There are all sorts of gates; famous ones like the Brandenburg gate in Germany, or common gates that surround homes or apartment complexes. In the natural, gates hide things, confine things, and even control things. Gates have the ability to allow, or prevent traffic to flow. Gates control mighty rivers allowing water in or out. Near Fresno, where I grew up, my family would go camping at Millerton Lake. Each summer we would make at least one trip to the base of Friant Dam. As I approached the bottom I could feel the mist and the power of the water passing through the gate. It was scary and exhilarating standing there near such massive power. Gates have more authority than we realize. Often they are taken for granted. Dr. Jonathan Alao tells the following story about a young man who *"Was being chased by a lion, he ran into his house and shut the gate that was protective. As he sat down to rest, he looked up and there was a Cobra looking down at him from the ceiling of the house, the same gate had become destructive."* Gates are essential to each one of us, they serve a purpose. Life is full of them.

The Wide Gate

Biblically there are two gates in each person's pathway. One is a narrow gate, and the other a wide gate. Let's focus on the wide gate first. The wide gate is the gate that leads to hell and eternal fire. Every person past the age of accountability (Deut. 1:39; James 4:17), who knows right from wrong, is on a crash course with this gate. This gate has a powerful draw to it. On the outside it is pleasing to the eye, but the inside is filled with pain and torment which lasts forever. This gate and the narrow one are locked in a battle for the soul of man. In Matthew 16:26 Jesus said, *"What profit is it to a man if he gains the whole world, and loses his own soul? Or what will a man give in exchange for his soul?"* Sadly mankind will give away the most important things in life to walk across the threshold of this gate. Unlike a husband on his wedding day carrying his bride across the threshold; man has exchanged their brides with temporary things. What could be more important than a relationship with God? Yet, trivial things go to the front of the line, ahead of God and heaven. The soul (eternal life) is far more valuable than the world.

Like a shiny lure on the end of a fishing line, the bait of Satan is set. With lies and deception at an all-time high, man chases after the beauty of the bait. Like rat poison, there is death mixed with enough truth to cloud judgment. So, unable to resist, the hook does it job, sinking deep into the flesh. Finally, the appeal of the world takes man thru the wide gate of death. For a while everything looks great and feels right, but eventually the hook draws blood; the pain becomes unbearable. Like a club to the head, dreams, goals and plans become a haze. Hope seems gone and rescue fleeting. The person at the end of the line is put in the net of sin and selfish living. From the net to the bucket becomes reality for all fish out of water. Trapped inside the spiritual bucket of death, becomes the norm. A wasted life flailing around, gasping for air, and in the end, death is waiting. This is life outside of the purpose of the Heavenly Father. Adam Clarke's Commentary on Habakkuk 1:14 affirms that God, *"Makes men as the fishes of the sea—easily taken and destroyed. We have no leader to guide us, and no power to defend ourselves."*

This gate is wide enough for every kind of evil, all religions, all political parties, and even has room for good people. All who will walk through this gate discard the truth (God's Word), exchanging it for the lies of Satan and the world's system. They are those who reject God's love through Jesus Christ. Sadly, this gate has claimed the souls of too many. Its victims become numb in the mind, body and spirit. They open themselves up to every kind of perversion and wickedness. As many remain silent, more and more pass through the gate and are destroyed. Unfortunately, the *"Gates of hell"* (Matt.

> *Like a shiny lure on the end of a fishing line, the bait of Satan is set.*

16.18) have wide nets and sharp hooks. More and more are being captured every day.

"Wide is the gate and broad is the way that leads to destruction, and there are many who go in by it" –Matthew 7:13

The Narrow Gate

There is hope, with God there is always hope. On the other side of the wide gate, only the love of God can make a difference. Only He can take the lost and hurting soul up and out of the net. Only a loving and forgiving Father is able to pull out the hook of sin, and set the sinner free. Amazingly, He pulls each floundering sinner, *"Saved by grace"* (Eph. 2:8-9) out the bucket of despair, into a new ocean. It's within new waters that everything changes. With another chance and new hope the Father reassures His catch saying, *"When you pass through the waters, I will be with you"* (Isa. 43:2).

Thankfully there is another gate; a way to be saved from the destruction the wide gate demands. In this book I call people to repentance; and say to the Christian community, "Wake up!" We cannot afford to sleep because the *"The days are evil"* (Eph. 5:16), we must make the most of each day. We must *"Arise...shine for all to see. For the glory of the Lord rises to shine on you"* (Isa. 60:1-2). We must lead as many as we can toward this gate; a gate of salvation. As the Heavenly Father draws them, we must lead them to Jesus who said, *"I am the gate. Those who come in through me will be saved"* (John 10:9 NLT). It's time to be bold and fearless, casting out God's nets of salvation. After all, we are *"Fishers of men"* (Matt. 4:19), and it's the Lord who knows where the lost fish are. Jesus said, *"Cast the net on the right side of the boat, and you will find some." So they cast, and now they were not able to draw it in because of the multitude of fish"* (John 21:6).

Those who love Jesus are the redeemed (Ps. 107:2). They live for Him as they walk the narrow road. Each one of us had to find the narrow gate on the broad road. That's right; on the highway to hell, there is a tiny, small opening. This gate offers a way off the broad road. The Bible says, *"There are few who find it"* (Matt. 7:14), but those who do will live forever. Those paying attention will find peace with God. Some found it as good people, doing very little selfish living. Others found it riddled with the hooks of sin pulling at them. While others found the narrow gate after they have fallen *"Away from the faith"* (1 Tim. 4:1). The narrow gate is for everyone. The fortunate find it and are blessed. It changes everything. I remember seeing it for the first time as an eight-year old. I hadn't lived long on the evil road, but long enough to know that I needed Jesus. I hadn't yet been hooked by life-altering sins, but still, He was offering a small child a better life. I learned later that Jesus was that little gate (John 10:9). As I grew up, I surrendered more of my heart to God. Then one day, I knew everything would be okay. I was blessed to accept Christ, the Rock early on. Jesus speaking about Himself said, *"On this rock I will build My church, and the gates of Hades shall not prevail against it"* (Matt. 16:18). It only takes one heart-felt decision to choose the narrow gate. All who do so have a source of power the world cannot offer. The old song by Edward Mote says it best, *"On Christ, the solid rock, I stand; all other ground is sinking sand."* It is the wise who build their lives upon the rock (Matt. 7:24), having power over hell's gates. Those who choose poorly sink beneath the waves and lose everything. Only the wise in Christ can withstand the power and lure of the wide gate. They will not be overcome by it. We must help others find the narrow gate and build a life upon Christ. It's the narrow gate which leads to ever-lasting life.

*"Narrow is the gate and difficult is the way which leads to
life, and there are few who find it" –Matthew 7:14*

The Narrow Road

Once we travel through Jesus (and Him alone), we begin down the narrow path which ultimately leads to eternal life. Not only do we travel through Jesus, but we must walk with Him daily. This way is difficult and requires commitment, determination, discipline, control, and even self-denial. It's a narrow road, with little space along its path. A person has to stay alert at all times lest he wander off its path and fall away. The narrow way requires the *"Mind of Christ"* (1 Cor. 2:16) because the road tests a man's thoughts. In the mind is where the real battle is. A Godly mind is essential because the heart, mind, body, and soul will be pushed to the limits. A double-minded man will struggle with each step, being *"Unstable in all his ways"* (James 1:8). Although this road is hard, and stumbling along the way is expected, help is ALWAYS a prayer of faith away. A faith-filled prayer *"Will save the sick, and the Lord will raise him up. And if he has committed sins, he will be forgiven"* (James 5:15). God is *"Our refuge and strength, A very present help in trouble"* (Psalm 46:1). Anyone can give their struggles and burdens to the Lord. This is one of the best aspects to this road. In fact, Jesus said, *"Come to Me, all you who labor and are heavy laden, and I will give you rest. Take My yoke upon you and learn from Me, for I am gentle and lowly in heart, and you will find rest for your souls. For My yoke is easy and My burden is light"* (Matt. 11:28-30). Life on the narrow road is a challenge, but there is nothing better or more satisfying than choosing to live for Christ. It is the highest call.

The Highway of Holiness

In Isaiah 35:8 the prophet gives the narrow road a name. He says, *"A highway shall be there, and a road, and it shall be called the Highway of Holiness. The unclean shall not pass over it, but it shall be for others. Whoever walks the road, although a fool, shall not go astray."* Holiness is essential to the sojourners on the narrow road. Without a high standard, God's standard, who said, *"Be holy because I am holy"* (1 Pet. 1:16), some will go astray.

The enemy constantly bombards us, shooting his *"Fiery darts"* (Eph.6:16). Although, this unrelenting attack slows and wounds the believer; a sincere faith is the remedy. For the soldier of Christ, faith is like a shield that will block the darts of the enemy.

A life of holy living guarantees the traveler that *"God is our refuge and strength, a very present help in trouble"* (Ps. 46:1). New believers, who have found their way off the wide road, have God's help in all circumstances and never need to be afraid. God the Father, and the Son, and the Holy Spirit are everywhere along the road showing all voyagers how to *"Press toward the goal for the prize of the upward call of God in Christ Jesus"* (Phil. 3:14). Whether in good seasons or during the trials and storms of life, those on this road can shine for Christ. In Matthew 7:1-29 there are six keys needed to thrive on this road:

- Key #1 – **Let God be the judge** (Vs. 1-6). Make sure you are seeing clearly, that nothing is blocking how you see yourself and others. Make sure you do not abuse what is holy, because you will be hurt in the process.
- Key #2 – **Keep asking, seeking, and knocking on God's door** (Vs. 7-12). God rewards persistency. Keep on asking God for the good things He offers. Learn what His will is, and then never get tired of wanting what He wants for your life, family, job and church.
- Key #3 – **The Narrow Way** (Vs. 13-14). Make sure you stay on the narrow road by living in holiness. Remember, *"For many are called but few are chosen"* (Matt. 22:14). Now, help others find the narrow path.
- Key #4 – **Watch your leaders carefully** (Vs. 15-20). Remain watchful because many leaders today should not be trusted. *"Their appearance and their claims are not proof of their true character"* (Bible Hub). It is important to connect with solid biblically based leaders.
- Key #5 – **An intimate relationship with Jesus is vital** (Vs. 21-23). There is a big difference between those who merely do things for Jesus, and those who know Him intimately. It's the difference of heaven and hell. Someone with a genuine relationship with Christ will *"Obey His commands"* (John 14:15).
- Key #6 – **Build your life upon Jesus the Rock** (Vs. 24-29). Only when you hear, learn and apply Jesus' Word (the Bible) to your life, are you on a good foundation. Foolish believers

are those who build parts of their life upon worldly foundations that crumble. When you face the storms of life, ONLY Jesus the Word of God, can save your soul and rescue you from people and the things that destroy.

> *"As you stand waiting for the Lord*
> *to open the next door in your life,*
> *strive to thrive on this side" -DLF*

Chapter 5 – The Broad Road

"All roads lead to your eternal home" –Danny Formhals Sr.

The people on this road

"All roads lead to Rome" is one the most ancient and popular phrases that we hear. Historically this was true at one time. When the Roman Empire ruled the known world at that time, the city of Rome was the center of life. Therefore, all roads led to the capital city, or led to roads that connect with them. The broad road is wide and at one time or another, all of us have traveled this road. This road has several lanes, and there are more people on this road today than at any other time in our history. With over seven billion people on the planet, most appear to dwell in and around its lanes. Some consider themselves safe on the narrow road, but the Holy Spirit speaks of many *"Fallen away from the faith"* (1 Tim. 4:1-3). It seems that few are talking about the millions who have wandered off the narrow road to join the masses on the broad one. The people on this road are lost and MUST be found. Oblivious to their deep need for Jesus Christ, they are convinced they are doing quite well. Jesus speaks about them saying, *"You are those who justify yourselves before men, but God knows your hearts. For what is highly esteemed among men is an abomination in the sight of God"* (Luke 16:15). We cannot forget that God is in control and *"It is the purpose of the Lord that will* stand" (Prov. 19:21). The God of the Bible knows the heart of man; He alone weighs motives, and understands why people do what they do. So anyone who lives on the broad road is being watched by the Father. For judgment (Duet. 1:17) and vengeance (Rom. 12:19) belong to the Lord. Our job is to love the people, warn them and leave the rest to the Lord. People are like trees. It is simple to determine whether a tree or a person is good or bad by the fruit produced. Jesus makes this clear in Matthew 7:17-18, *"Even so, every good tree bears good fruit, but a bad tree bears bad fruit. A good tree cannot bear bad fruit, nor can a bad tree bear good fruit."* Regardless of what we see, it is God's responsibility to judge eternal life, not ours.

Ignoring the coming destruction

All roads lead to your eternal home. Some *"Will go away into everlasting punishment, but the righteous into eternal life"* (Matt. 25:46). I cannot help but shake my head in wonder at what Christianity and the local church has become. It boggles my mind that preachers and people who claim to love the Word of God, take heaven and especially hell for granted. I am not a fire and brimstone preacher, but I do preach on hell, sin and judgment. Take John 3:16, undoubtedly the most popular Bible verse. It reads, *"For God so loved the world that He gave His only begotten Son, that whoever believes in Him should not perish but have everlasting life."* This verse has it all:

- **LOVE** – The character of God, His great love for us and the whole world.
- **JESUS CHRIST** – The Son of God who died for our sins.
- **BELIEVE** – The way to relationship with God, through His Son.

- **DESTRUCTION** – The very thing God wants to save us from, perishing in the lake of fire.
- **ETERNAL LIFE** – The very thing God want to give us, heaven.

Hidden in between the most-read Bible verse in history are sin, judgment and even hell. It is impossible to preach on God's love without speaking to why He loves us. Things are changing for the worst when Christian leaders see *"Love"* in scripture and not the reason for it. God's love came to save people from destruction. Many local churches and leaders have become *"The blind leading the blind"* (Matt. 15:14). Blind guides are everywhere. They love God and preach His word powerfully, some have big followings, but are unaware they are in danger of setting God's people up for disappointment. Preaching on sin and hell isn't some scare tactic, putting people under a so-called unbiblical weight. Seeing God's love and holiness should, in fact, help us

> *It is impossible to preach on God's love without speaking to why He loves us.*

see the sin in our lives. In Luke 5:1-11 Jesus asked Simon (Peter) to *"Launch out into the deep and let down your nets for a catch"* (Luke 5:4). He complained saying, *"Master, we have toiled all night and caught nothing; nevertheless at Your word I will let down the net"* (Luke 5:5). At once the nets were full; the catch was so huge the boat almost sank, Peter *"Fell down at Jesus' knees, saying, "Depart from me, for I am a sinful man, O Lord"* (Luke 5:8). Peter saw the power and love of God and it drove him to his knees. In the middle of it all, Peter saw his sin. Why didn't Jesus stop him and say, "Get up Peter, I just wanted you to know I love you." The Bible says, *"When they had brought their boats to land, they forsook all and followed Him"*

(Luke 5:11). Today, we want people to know God loves them without harping about sin, hell, and judgment. Jesus exposed our weakness, sin and wrong motives, and people forsook (abandoned) all and followed him, because they loved Him. What a difference!

We cannot forget the obvious

Now, step back and view the Word of God from a distance. Few could argue the story from Genesis to Revelation is a call to turn away from evil (repent), follow God, and love His people. The truth is obvious, in black and white, in the pages of scripture. In Genesis the world was destroyed by water. *"The waters prevailed exceedingly on the earth, and all the high hills under the whole heaven were covered* (Gen. 7:19-23). It was a world-wide flood. On the other end of scripture, Revelation 21:1 speaks of another world-wide event, *"Now I saw a new heaven and a new earth, for the first heaven and the first earth had passed away. Also there was no more sea."* This event is prophesied throughout the Bible, here is Peter's description of it, *"The heavens will pass away with a great noise, and the elements will melt with fervent heat; both the earth and the works that are in it will be burned up"* (2 Pet. 3:10). Plainly, the beginning, the ending and all the way through, the Bible speaks about destruction. Yet, our elected leaders, believers or unbelievers, inside the church or outside, choose to ignore these essential messages.

The Apostle Peter exposes *"Last Days"* *"Scoffers"* and exposes them as those *"Who willfully forget."* These leaders have overlooked what Almighty God did to the earth in Genesis and what He is planning to do in Revelation. Preachers and teachers today who avoid warning congregations about what the Father

Danny L. Formhals Sr.

said is coming, is a failure to their calling. Willful or not, it is one of the greatest mistakes being made today. Sadly, many of our shepherds and leaders are unintentionally caught up in a wave of deception sweeping through the church. They are ignorant and do not know the Word, which is bad enough. While this is a major disservice to the ministry, those purposely leading God's people astray are playing at a whole different level. Regardless, when any of God's chosen ministers hurt His people, judgment is coming. Whether in churches, school yards, state capitols, or in Washington DC, leaders will regret lying about God's Word. Here is what Peter said about these ministers and leaders in the last days.

"Beloved, I now write to you this second epistle (in both of which I stir up your pure minds by way of reminder), ² that you may be mindful of the words which were spoken before by the holy prophets, and of the commandment of us, the apostles of the Lord and Savior, ³ knowing this first: that scoffers will come in the last days, walking according to their own lusts, ⁴ and saying, "Where is the promise of His coming? For since the fathers fell asleep, all things continue as they were from the beginning of creation." ⁵ For this they willfully forget: that by the word of God the heavens were of old, and the earth standing out of water and in the water, ⁶ by which the world that then existed perished, being flooded with water. ⁷ But the heavens and the earth which are now preserved by the same word, are reserved for fire until the day of judgment and perdition of ungodly men" -2 Peter 3:1-7

Everlasting Punishment

The road to everlasting punishment is like a European autobahn, moving at blazing speeds. Usually in times of war the main roads are deserted (Isa. 33:8), but not in this case. Like the Great Barrier Reef off the coast of Australia, this road is teeming with life. The simplest way to say it is, the broad road is bad, and

64

the narrow road is good. The plain truth, which many refuse to preach with conviction is, *"Every tree that does not bear good fruit is cut down and thrown into the fire"* (Matt. 7:19). One day, the divine gardener will come to clean up

this road. The Father loves His garden, *"For joy and gladness will be found in her"* (Isa. 51:3). As ministers which we all are, God has hired us with a holy calling, to tend to and care for His garden (Matt. 20:1-16). In these final years before the return of the Lord, it is becoming harder to recognize the tares from the wheat. One day, God will send the reapers to gather those on this road and throw them in the fire. In the Parable of the Wheat and Tares Jesus said:

> *"The kingdom of heaven is like a man who sowed good seed in his field; but while men slept, his enemy came and sowed tares among the wheat and went his way. But when the grain had sprouted and produced a crop, then the tares also appeared. So the servants of the owner came and said to him, 'Sir, did you not sow good seed in your field? How then does it have tares?' He said to them, 'An enemy has done this.' The servants said to him, 'Do you want us then to go and gather them up?' But he said, 'No, lest while you gather up the tares you also uproot the wheat with them. Let both grow together until the harvest, and at the time of harvest I will say to the reapers, "First gather together the tares and bind them in bundles to burn them, but gather the wheat into my barn."-Matthew 13:24-30*

Danny L. Formhals Sr.

Are we leading people astray?

People have so many roadblocks in front of them. Spotting the narrow gate is becoming more and more challenging. It's there, but it hard to see. Our hearts should break because the overall Body of Christ (the world-wide church), is filled with fake ministers of righteousness. Some occupy pulpits, while some with Reverend in front of their name spew hate and anti-biblical sentiments. Today, it seems that anyone can become a Reverend. As walking into a chicken coup doesn't make you anymore able to lay eggs; nor does the title reverend next to a name make you a preacher of righteousness. Jesus gave us clues to recognize them. He said, *"You will know them by their fruits"* (Matt. 7:16).

These and other so-called Christian leaders are merely phony ministers of righteousness. Washington DC loves to harbor them also. Many of our political leaders, in all three branches of government say, "I am a Christian." This means, they claim to represent Christ. Yet, they champion obvious evil and anti-biblical laws. They were chosen and elected to serve the people; instead, they chose to serve themselves, a political party and Satan himself. We may not recognize them all, but they are of no surprise to the Lord. *"For such are false apostles, deceitful workers, transforming themselves into apostles of Christ. And no wonder! For Satan himself transforms himself into an angel of light. Therefore it is no great thing if his ministers also transform themselves into ministers of righteousness, whose end will be according to their works"* (2 Cor. 11:13-15).

One preacher said, "Some of them are possessed by Satan. They purposely twist the Word of God and lie to the people as Satan lied to Eve. Some of them are like Eve, without knowing they serve the cause of Satan." When leaders, spiritual or not tell people, "Don't worry, everything is going to be okay", watch out. When the Body of Christ has been infiltrated with those who state, "God isn't going to send anyone to hell, in fact there isn't even a hell to worry about", we're living dangerously. Often with good intentions, they twist scriptures to put their congregants and the people at ease. The Reformation Study Bible says, "Presenting a rosy picture of the Christian life and minimizing that it is filled with trouble does not follow the lead of our Lord." In Acts the early church leaders had it right. Life was hard for them. The Christian life is supposed to be hard at times. The early church leaders were, *"Strengthening the souls of the disciples, exhorting them to continue in the faith, and saying, "We must through many tribulations enter the kingdom of God"* (Acts 14:22).

The broad road is extremely dangerous. It encompasses all evil and deception. The worst kind of trouble waits all who travel its eight lanes. The Bible calls it *"The Way that leads to destruction"* (Matt. 7:13). Living in America, in her moral decline, doesn't make it easy to exit off the broad road. The true Christian is disappearing, which doesn't help the lost find their way off the road. The outright lies and deception in the public area is shocking. Inside the red, white and blue is plenty of space for selfishness as well. Self-serving makes room for every category of problems imaginable. The people on the broad road deal with their problems by blame. Accepting responsibility isn't new to the game, just ask Adam and Eve. Today, the issue has grown exponentially. When life goes wrong, it's someone or something else's fault. This has led to an entitlement culture, which has become the accepted cultural norm.

Like litter on the side of the road, its shoulders are complete with piles of distractions. Everything necessary to take hearts and mind off Christ and His Word are found flooding these streets. Just one moment of disorder and distraction is enough to send the people speeding away from the love of God and what really matters. The broad way is the way of the un-thoughtful, the undisciplined, the lazy, the worldly, the ungodly, the materialistic, and the carnal. The Bible says, *"There is a way that SEEMS right to a man, but its end is the way of death"* (Prov. 16:25; 14:12).

What really disturbs me are the countless CINO people who refuse to preach all truth. If the gospel was being preached, the fools who drive these lanes would find Christ and His narrow gate. Sadly, they don't hear it because generally speaking, Christians aren't preaching it. Our society is all the proof needed to know that too many are on the wide road that leads to destruction. Here are some shocking statistics about life on the wide-road.

Life on the Wide Road

- **America is going in the wrong direction** – 81% of Americans in a recent poll said this nation is on the wrong track (*New York Times/ CBS News poll April 2008*).

- **Dependency on government** – According to the U.S. Census Bureau the poverty rate is now 15% or 46.5 million people living in poverty today. People are making less today than in 2008. Currently, 47.6 million Americans are on food stamps (FNS.USDA.GOV). In recent years a fundamental shift has befallen the United States. Somewhere along the way we have traded our dependency on the God of the Bible to the Federal Government. God is no longer the source. Instead, dependency on the government is at an all-time high. According to the Census Bureau, 49 percent of all American households get direct monetary benefits from the federal government. Back in 1983, less than a third of all American households received aid from the federal government. It true, most families need a helping hand from time to time. The problem today is; the government is becoming our hope and provider, not Almighty God. This nation is overstepping its boundaries. If things continue to spiral downward, the *"Government simply won't be able to pay for all the things it has promised"* (Time.com).

- **Religion is in decline** – The number of Americans who consider religion not to be very important has quadrupled in the last 50 years. A Gallop poll says that 40% of Americans attend church. While the numbers are on serious decline, Churchleaders.com has an article disputing the numbers. They state that the number is actually about half that; 20%. They discovered that most pastors acknowledge 40%-60% of their people are considered inactive members. They go on to classify a regular attendee as someone who shows up at least three out of every eight Sundays, only 23%-25% of Americans would fit this category (Churchleaders.com). The local church is fighting to survive in many cases.

- **Crime** – In 2013 according to Newsmax.com, violent crime is up 15%, while the property crime rate rose by 12% in the United States. The evidence is proving, what many already believe, that crime is beginning to trend upward. "By the 1990's, the U.S. was opening on average one new prison or jail every week. Today, the United States has the largest prison population in the world and the highest incarcerations rate in the world" (Justice Policy Institute). America is a young nation, only 238 years old. Research shows that it took America about 160 years to confine its first 1 million criminals. Just twelve more years to imprison the 2nd million criminals. In a published study in Crime and Delinquency, "By the age 23, 49% of black males and 38% of white males have been arrested." There is always hope with God. Hebrews 13:3 says, *"Remember the prisoners as if chained with them."*

- **Abortion** – America is murdering and devaluing what God created; life. Jesus said, *"For He is not the God of the dead but of the living, for all live to Him"* (Luke 20:38). According to the National Right to Life, each year, Americans abort roughly 1.2 million babies. Most are killed in the name of convenience. Make no mistake about it, biblically, abortion is sin. I will cover this subject in greater detail in chapter six, lane five.

- **Alternative Lifestyles** – America is becoming more open and accepting to how people choose to live their lives. Gay rights have become a major hot-button issue in America. Alternative lifestyles are generally perceived to be outside the social norms. These norms are changing drastically. One that smacks in the face of Biblical doctrine is same-sex marriage. This new alternative lifestyle is gaining tremendous ground in the United States. It has become legal in 17 U.S. States and the District of Columbia and in 16 other countries worldwide (CNN). While support for homosexuality is swelling, the Bible is clear and condemns the practice (Lev. 18:22; 20:13; 1 Cor. 6:9-10; Rom. 1:18-32). Few talk about the fact that homosexuality is God's judgment upon societies and nations who continue to reject and acknowledge His love for them. In his song *America Again*, Christian artist Carman says, "When we'd rather come out of the closet then clean it, it's a sign that judgment is going to fall." The world needs to be reminded what the Bible says about these lifestyles. While He loves all, and wants what is best, He declares, *"The wrath of God is revealed from heaven against all ungodliness and unrighteousness of men, who suppress the truth in unrighteousness* (Romans 1:18). I will cover this subject in greater detail in chapter six, lane four.

- **Marriage** – The institute of marriage wasn't created by human beings. Rather, marriage was a divine idea to connect male and female together. Marriage is undergoing changes because society has decided that God's way isn't best. The Bible speaks to motherhood, widows, and women in general, not single parenthood; this was never God's plan. God said regarding marriage, *"It is not good that the man should be alone; I will make him a helper fit for him"* (Gen. 2:20). In the six-day creation account, God repeatedly identified that His creation was good (see Genesis 1:4, 10, 12, 18, 21, 25, 31). Of all He created, man was not yet complete. So, God created the woman, to be united with the man and become *"One flesh."* (Gen. 2:24). Today, even believers have forgotten, *"God hates divorce"* (Mal. 2:15-16).

The divorce rate is nearly the same between Christians and non-believers. One preacher said, "I've never met a couple who divorced because they were pursuing God too much." Speaking of marriage Jesus said, *"What God has joined together, let no man separate"* (Mark 10:5-9). Sadly, secular progressives have partnered with Satan who is bent on destroying marriage. This has hurt the church and the nation. The destruction of the family unit and marriage is crystal clear. In 1950, 78% of households were occupied by married couples. Currently, that number has dropped to 48%. Until God intervenes, this will continue to cause irreparable harm to the children and teenagers in America. Statistically, *"A child in a single-parent household is far more likely to experience violence, commit suicide, continue a cycle of poverty, become drug dependent, commit a crime or perform below his peers in education"* (Single Parent Success Foundation). Children are told, *"Obey your parents in the Lord, for this is right"* (Eph. 6:1).

* **The Drug and Alcohol Epidemic** – According to the CDC, the Centers for Disease Control and Prevention, "There are approximately 88,000 deaths attributable to excessive alcohol use each year in the United States. This is the third leading lifestyle-related cause of death for the nation." Couple that with the massive rise of drug use and this epidemic is out of control. It is no secret that this epidemic is blatantly out in the open. Twenty states plus the District of Columbia allow the use medical marijuana. In 2013 two states; Washington and Colorado voted to legalize the use of recreational Marijuana. This has opened a can of deadly worms and is a direct slap in the face of God and His Word.

Marijuana, united with alcohol, is destroying the will of man to follow God.

- **Pornography** – This foul and immoral industry is single-handedly destroying the minds our nation's men and boys. Pornography addicts are in bondage; they are slaves in the prison of their mind. The Bible instructs us to *"Flee lust"* (2 Tim. 2:22) and *"Flee fornication"* (1 Cor. 6:18). The Bible calls pornography a sin against one's own body (1 Cor. 6:18-20). "Americans spend more than $10 billion a year on porn" (O'Reilly Factor, Fox News). The Pornography Statistics Annual Report for 2013 reveals some very shocking numbers: (1) 50% of all Christian men say they are addicted to porn. (2) 51% of pastors say Internet porn is a possible temptation. (3) 71% of teens hide online behavior from parents. (4) 83% of boys and 57% of girls have seen group sex online. (5) 64% of college men go online weekly for Internet sex. (6) 67% of young men and 49% of young women think porn is an appropriate way to express one's sexuality. (7) 56% of divorces are due to one party's involved in porn. Societies crumble from within because of sexual immorality. America's days are numbered, unless we repent and turn back to the Lord.

- **Biblical Foundation** – The founding fathers established this union and collection of states upon several Biblical principles. Especially the judicial system, America's way, comes from the Word of God. Everything, including nations, survives on strong, solid foundations. Whether, hearts, homes, or societies, *"If the foundations are destroyed, what can the righteous do?"* (Ps. 11:3). Like a rug being pulled out from underneath a man, the Bible is slowly and methodically being eroded away from America. Without a solid foundation, evil will be left to rule the day. America as a force for good in the world will be left to corrupt and selfish nations like Russian and Iran. It's up to individuals to stand upon principals. Sadly, the nation's passion for the Word of God is losing precious ground. In a recent survey, 66 percent of those surveyed said the Bible contains everything a person needs to know to live a meaningful life. But, 58 percent of those said they don't actually want the wisdom and advice given from Scripture (2013 State of the Bible Survey by the Barna Group). America is doomed unless she gets back to her Biblical roots.

Where have the watchmen gone?

Watchmen are a dying breed. Too many have left their post of protection. The very call of God to tend, care for and watch over the sheep (John 21:16-17), has been neglected. Too many have stopped looking for the enemy; allowing him to come in secretly. The walls of Christianity are broken and exposed to attack. The wolves, the skeptics and scoffers of the end-times have crept into the Body of Christ and are deceiving many. Where have all the watchmen gone?

When 58% of believers don't want the truth, it is a clear sign that judgment is coming.

This book is a warning call. The local church, the Body of Christ is being overrun by sleeping, lazy and apathetic believers. Ephesians 5:14 is a call to *"Awaken from your sleep."* The church in Ephesus was warned to watch, *"Redeeming the time, because the days are evil"* (Eph. 5:16). Watchers are those who are awake and paying attention. Their eyes are scanning the horizon for the attack of the enemy. If ever there was a time to recognize the evil around us, today is that day. There is an urgency to warn the people about what is coming. I feel it strongly. Sadly, too many are blinded to the all-out assault upon Jesus and His church. Americans see the decline of morals around them. Most people, religious or not, sense something is about to break. Commentators; spiritual or not, are speaking about America and the world being at a tipping point. Not enough is being done to wake up the masses. Believers know the solution is the Word of God, which is why many run to the church after a disaster. When 58% of believers don't want the truth, it is a clear sign that judgment is coming. It's like seeing the hole on a sinking ship and refusing to put your finger in to plug it up. The ship is the believer and the church, the hole is sin, the water is the world and the passengers are spiritual and political leaders.

Today, too many Christians and their leaders are watching the water come pouring into the ship. Don't be deceived, the ship is going to sink until God steps in to save us. Like the Midianites who invaded the land of Israel, we have our own invaders. Like locusts they came into Israel to destroy and plunder it. Previously, the people had peace for forty years (Judges 5:31), but somehow they let down their guard. When the watchers left their places *"The children of Israel did evil in the sight of the Lord. So the Lord delivered them into the hand of Midian for seven years, and the hand of Midian prevailed against Israel"* (Judges 6:1-2). All God's people could do was hide in dens and caves, leaving the land vulnerable. The Bible says, *"Israel was greatly impoverished because of the Midianites"* (Judges 6:6). Israel, in the Old Testament is a type and shadow of the things that plague the New Testament church today.

Because of our sin and unwillingness to wake up, our churches, our doctrine and our power are weakening. Many houses of worship have become a *"Den of thieves"* (Matt. 21:13), changing into something other than *"A house of prayer"* (Matt. 21:13). Our homes

> *Many houses of worship have become a den of thieves!*

have become caves devoid of God's Word and ways. Like the people of Israel, we have lost sight of who we are in Christ. Our loss of biblical identity has given the enemy, great pleasure in redefining us. Our own Midianites have driven us into hiding. Our boat is sinking, our walls are unmanned, and local church is impoverished. All of this was predicted in scripture as the *"Great falling*

away" (2 Thess. 2:1-3). So, where are all the watchmen? Where are the spiritual voices? Who are representing God and His Word to the world? Have they fallen away? God needs His people on the wall. Those who will boldly declare what Coronel Jessup said in the movie, *A Few Good Men*. He said, "You want me on that wall; you need me on that wall!"

Like the children of Israel who *"Cried out to the Lord"* (Judges 6:7), we must do the same. Until the heart and souls of believers are awakened by the Holy Spirit, the truth will continue to be suppressed. Until we open our eyes to the darkness which is growing, and get back up on the wall, the warning will continue to fall on deaf ears. When we finally cry out to the Lord, He will raise up a Gideon. One day, the Lord God Almighty will turn and say, *"Go in this might of yours, and you shall save Israel from the hand of the Midianites"* (Judges 6:14). I believe the Gideon's will rise up from those who are watching and praying. In the New Testament, we are called to be watchers.

- **Matthew 24:42** – *"Watch therefore, for you do not know what hour your Lord is coming."*
- **Matthew 25:13** – *"Watch therefore, for you know neither the day nor the hour in which the Son of Man is coming."*
- **Mark 13:33** – *"Take heed, watch and pray; for you do not know when the time is."*
- **Mark 13:35-37** – *"Watch therefore, for you do not know when the master of the house is coming--in the evening, at midnight, at the crowing of the rooster, or in the morning--lest, coming suddenly, he find you sleeping. And what I say to you, I say to all: Watch!"*
- **Acts 20:31** – *"Therefore watch, and remember that for three years I did not cease to warn everyone night and day with tears."*
- **1 Corinthians 16:13** – *"Watch, stand fast in the faith, be brave, be strong."*
- **1 Thessalonians 5:6** – *"Therefore let us not sleep, as others do, but let us watch and be sober."*
- **Revelation 3:2-3** – *"Be watchful, and strengthen the things which remain, that are ready to die, for I have not found your works perfect before God. Remember therefore how you have received and heard; hold fast and repent. Therefore if you will not watch, I will come upon you as a thief, and you will not know what hour I will come upon you."*

Watching and warning the city

Like the prophet Ezekiel, called to be a watchmen over Israel, God has spoken to the spiritual leaders today. If we don't stand watch; in our homes, neighborhoods, cities and nations, who will? God is saying to us, *"I have made you a watchman...therefore hear a word from My mouth, and give them warning from Me"*

(Ez. 3:17). Like the prophet Isaiah watching over the city of Jerusalem (Isa. 62:6), I believe God is looking for watchmen to stand guard over our cities. A watchman takes responsibility to care for God's people. A watchman is dedicated to the welfare of the people; to pray for them, to deliver the Word of the Lord, to help the people be successful. A watchman sounds the warning when the enemy is coming. Where are the watchmen today? The success of the city has everything to do with the righteous. Psalm 11:10-11 says, *"When it goes well with the righteous, the city rejoices; And when the wicked perish, there is jubilation. By the blessing of the upright the city is exalted, But it is overthrown by the mouth of the wicked."*

Speaking about the end-times, the fig tree budding (which is Israel), and the final generation, Jesus said, *"But take heed to yourselves, lest your hearts be weighed down with carousing, drunkenness, and cares of this life, and that Day come on you unexpectedly. For it will come as a snare on all those who dwell on the face of the whole earth. Watch therefore, and pray always that you may be counted worthy to escape all these things that will come to pass, and to stand before the Son of Man"* (Luke 21:34-36). Ever since this great country was founded, a warning has been sounded. Since the early years of America, many voices have warned us. In 1779 Samuel Adams wrote: *"A general dissolution of principles and manners will more surely overthrow the liberties of America than the whole force of the common enemy. While the people are virtuous they cannot be subdued; but when once they lose their virtue then will be ready to surrender their liberties to the first external or internal invader."*

There are two groups of people; those who need to hear the warning, and those who need to proclaim it. Which are you? The broad road will continue to destroy and lead people away from the Lord. This means the warning must rise above the noise and distractions. This means we must be louder than the enemy. The Word of God has been declared, the watchmen are appointed, and the enemy is here. Somebody will be held responsible for those lost to this road. Make no mistake about it; the blood will be upon someone's head.

The Warning!

Again the word of the Lord came to me, saying, "Son of man, speak to the children of your people, and say to them: 'When I bring the sword upon a land, and the people of the land take a man from their territory and make him their watchman, when he sees the sword coming upon the land, if he blows the trumpet and warns the people, then whoever hears the sound of the trumpet and does not take warning, if the sword comes and takes him away, his blood shall be on his own head. He heard the sound of the trumpet, but did not take warning; his blood shall be upon himself. But he who takes warning will save his life. But if the watchman sees the sword coming and does not blow the trumpet, and the people are not warned, and the sword comes and takes any person from among them, he is taken away in his iniquity; but his blood I will require at the watchman's hand.' "So you, son of man: I have made you a watchman for the house of Israel; therefore you shall hear a word from My mouth and warn them for Me. - Ezekiel 33:1-7

> *"People on earth hate to hear the word REPENT! Those in hell wish they could hear it just once more"* -Unknown

Chapter 6 – The 8-Lane Highway

"The road to hell is paved with good intentions." – Saint Bernard of Clairvaux

The Broad Road is the Eight Land Highway

When I came to pastor the Abundant Life Center church in 2005, I was young, a new pastor and pastoring my first church. Roy Bay was one of the senior saints in the congregation. One day he walked into the local Denny's Restaurant as I was having coffee. I invited him to sit down and soon after it became a regular thing. We would talk about the Bible, the good old days, and the church. He loved to talk about the end-times, me too. Quickly, we hit it off. I loved hanging out with brother Bay, as I called him. He was one of the early friendships I developed in Humboldt County. He has since passed on to be with the Lord. I miss him and often reflect on his words about the good old days when church life was more black and white, simpler than it is today.

One day he asked me if I had ever heard of the *8-Lane Highway*. I hadn't, so for the next hour he shared with me what the Lord had given him years before. Shortly thereafter, with Roy's blessing, I preached a sermon series titled, *the 8-Lane Highway*. Several years later, the Lord impressed upon me to write this book. I want to thank brother Roy Bay, who is in heaven for his inspiration. Here is the verse brother Bay shared with me.

Revelation 21:8
"The cowardly, unbelieving, abominable, murderers, sexually immoral, sorcerers, idolaters, and all liars shall have their part in the lake which burns with fire and brimstone, which is the second death."

This verse speaks of eight sins leading to the lake of fire, and the second death. The first death is physical death (Matt. 10:28). Those who die without Christ are doomed to face the second death, when the spiritually dead are *"Cast into the lake of fire"* (Rev. 20:14). The unfortunate who die on the *8-Lane Highway*, never finding the narrow gate, become eternally separated from God (2 Thess. 1:9). They are the unsaved and *"Unbelievers"* (2 Cor. 6:14). Fortunate are those who find Christ and the narrow road. The Bible says, *"Blessed and holy is he who has part in the first resurrection. Over such the second death has no power, but they shall be priests of God and of Christ, and shall reign with Him a thousand years"* (Rev. 20:6). Make no mistake about it; the broad road is the *8-Lane Highway*. These lanes, these sins, are life-styles. All people, in Christ or apart for Him, must be fore-warned. Destruction awaits all who live or dabble on this road. The victims of sin, which pulls us away from God, end up traveling on the lanes of this highway.

The Cowardly

Proverbs 29:25 (NKJV)
*"The fear of man brings a snare,
But whoever trusts in the LORD
shall be safe."*

LANE
1

Lane One – The COWARDLY

Like the cowardly lion in the Wizard of Oz, these travelers live in fear. Afraid to move, take risks and use their gifting's for God, they become useless. The Kingdom of God cannot advance unless brave warriors having the right energy and dedication can *"Take it by force"* (Matt. 11:12). Individual salvation is the goal of Christ's Kingdom. Success greatly depends on men and women who understand how to give *"All their cares"* and fears to the Lord (Ps. 55:22). Sadly, too many have become like a captain who abandons his ship before all the people are safe. That man is a coward and lives in fear.

Speaking to the power of fear in a believer, Rick Renner in his article *The Things Christians Fear* explains, "If fear gets into your mind, you won't want to face anything; thus, it will produce cowardice in you. You will be afraid to get out of bed, afraid to go to work, afraid to make vital decisions, afraid of everything and everyone. If you allow it to do so, fear will eventually control your life." He's right, when fear grips true believers, they become wounded and ineffective. When fear slips into the local church, it becomes a place which turns the stomach of God (Rev. 3:14-22).

> There are 365 "Fear not's" in the Bible, one for every day of the year

While fear is a common factor all people face, true Christians must rise above it. God's Word is a book of promises. *SoulShephardign.org* says, "Fear not!" is the most repeated command in the Bible. In fact, it's been said that there are 365 "Fear not's" in the Bible — one "Fear not" for every day of the year! In fact, Lloyd Ogilvie in *Facing the Future without Fear* said there are 366 "Fear not's" in the Bible, one for every day of the year, including Leap Year! God doesn't want us to go a single day without hearing his word of comfort, "Fear not!" Some common fears believers struggle with are:

- **Living in Pain** – God promised to help us through the pain (Ps. 34:8), yet fear has caused us to ignore the Word of God which brings comfort (Job 6:10).
- **Being Ashamed** – God promised to give us power and authority (Luke 10:19), yet fear has caused us to be *"Ashamed of the Gospel"* (Rom. 1:16).
- **Being Rejection** – God promised to make us complete in Him (Col. 2:10), yet fear has caused us to focus on what is against us, not for us (Rom. 8:31).
- **Uncertainty** – God promised to meet our needs (Phil. 4:19), yet fear has caused many to trust in man instead of God, looking else ware for help (Ps. 118:8).
- **Being Opposing by Others** – God promised to fight for us (Duet. 20:4), yet fear has caused us to forget that we have a great God inside (1 John 4:4).
- **Looking Stupid** – God promised to give us confidence (1 John 5:14), yet fear has caused us to struggle when offenses come (Matt. 18:7-10).
- **Failure** – God promised we could be great in the Kingdom of God (Matt. 18:4), yet fear has caused us to focus on our mistakes and not overcome them (1 Cor. 10:12).
- **Judgment** – God promised that judgment would come (2 Cor. 5:10), yet fear has caused us to not get right with Him and even do what is right (Is. 1:17).

- **The past** – God promised to make us new (2 Cor. 5:17), yet fear has kept us from *"Forgetting those things with are behind"* and pressing on toward Godly goals (Phil. 3:9-10).
- **Death** – God promised to give us life (John 10:10), and eternal life (2 Tim. 1:10), yet fear has kept us from experiencing the blessings of God (Gal. 3:13-14).
- **Financial problems** – God promised to provide those who give (Luke 6:38), yet fear has keep many from experiencing and understanding the principal of sowing and reaping (2 Cor. 9:9).
- **Spiritual Attacks** – God promised to help us resist the Devil (1 Pet. 5:9-10), yet fear has caused us to *"Wrestle with flesh and blood"* instead (Eph. 6:12).

Jason Bradley said, "Truly trusting God means that we, of all people, should be running toward the uncertain, precarious areas of life. We should be the most courageous, audacious, and resolute people on the planet." This is a very difficult accomplishment for those living and running in this lane. The cowardly and fearful don't realize they were created for the glory of the Lord (Isa. 43:7). They don't believe they were made to be God's workmanship, and to do good works (Eph. 2:10). These people live for themselves and want to be safe from harm's way.

Cowards rarely take risks, so it becomes easy to put Christ on the back shelf. Their Christianity becomes a passing fad. They never share their faith for fear of being called a radical, a Jesus-freak, or something worse. They like to hide in the shadows and don't want to be seen or shine for Christ. Their Christianity is personal and they resent anyone who expects them to be a witness for Christ. They frequently take the easy way out and often blame others for their problems. Today, cowards don't want to give up the world, because it has become safe for them. Worst of all they never confess their sins. Cowards lack courage to do dangerous or unpleasant things for God. They cannot grasp the concept of endurance. When the preacher says, *"He who endures to the end shall be saved"* (Matt. 24:13), they don't get it. So, they remain lukewarm, and many become lost. They live like zombies, dead men, because they have denied the Lord on earth. Therefore, there is no real life inside.

This lane is perfect for those who fear taking a stand for Christ. Matthew 10:32-33 declares, *"Therefore whoever confesses Me before men, him I will also confess before My Father who is in heaven. But whoever denies Me before men, him I will also deny before My Father who is in heaven."* Fearing to act, or step out in faith, is a very strong reason many lack confidence and courage to stand up for Christ. Today, the wrong kind of fear is dismantling Christian foundations. Therefore, too many opt for the cowards' life instead of the new life God promises.

Hebrews 10:19-24 speaks to those who live by faith and experience a new life in Christ. Further down the chapter, Hebrews 10:25-29 speaks to those who fail to *"Draw near to God."* There are four things I want to point out regarding this group. (1) In verse 25 they stop going to church. Here the cowardly walk away from the people of God and therefore disobey God's command to not forsake *"The assembling of ourselves together."* (2) In verse 26 they continue to sin even though they *"Received the knowledge of the truth."* This willful and deliberate act is equal to apostasy; which is walking away from the faith. (3) In verse 27 their actions are cowardly because they literally reject God's greatest gift of salvation having a certain *"Expectation of judgment."* (4) In verse

29 the punishment for them as they *"trampled the Son of God underfoot"* will be severe. Their actions reduce the blood of Christ to a common thing, which is an insult to God's grace.

Fear is a powerful ally of the enemy. Striking fear in the enemy is a military tactic that has been around forever. This is undoubtedly one of the reasons the United States of America dropped the first atomic bombs on Japan's Hiroshima and three days later on Nagasaki. In November 1987, In the *Omaha World Herald* is an article that sheds light on what many didn't know concerning War World II. "Deep in the recesses of the National Archives in Washington, D.C., hidden for nearly four decades lie thousands

of pages of yellowing and dusty documents stamped 'Top Secret'.

These documents, now declassified, are the plans for Operation Downfall, the invasion of Japan during World War II. Only a few Americans in 1945 were aware of the elaborate plans that had been prepared for the Allied Invasion of the Japanese home islands. Even fewer today are aware of the defenses the Japanese had prepared to counter the invasion had it been launched. Operation Downfall was finalized during the spring and summer of 1945. It called for two massive military undertakings to be carried out in succession and aimed at the heart of the Japanese Empire." It was believed that once the invasion began, some 1,000 Japanese and American troops would die every hour.

The invasion of Japan never became a reality because on the morning of August 6, 1945, the American B-29 bomber, the 'Enola Gay' dropped the first ever atomic bomb by parachute. It floated down exploding 1,900 feet above the ground. Between 60,000 and 80,000 were killed instantly. It was reported that many just vanished because of the intense heat. The final death toll was 135,000. The second and bigger bomb destroyed a third of the city of Nagasaki and killed about 50,000 people. Within days after the bombings, the war with Japan was at a close. The world was spared the end-result of Operation Downfall. On September 2, 1945 Japan formally surrendered to the United Nations, and World War II was over. The fear those bombs enacted, probably saved the lives of millions if the war had gone on. The above article was titled, *How the Atomic Bomb Saved 4,000,000 Lives.*

Fear has two sides; a dark side and God's side. One is the *"Spirit of fear"* (2 Tim 1:7), and the other is *"The fear of the Lord"* (Ps. 111:10). One leads to cowardly living while the other brings understanding and wisdom. The dark side of fear can be overcome. When the fearful begin thinking and applying more of God's love fear is dissolved. First, John 4:18 says, *"Perfect love casts out fear."*

The Dark Side of Fear

F – THE FRIGHTFUL FEAR: Judges 7:3 *"Proclaim in the hearing of the people, saying, 'Whoever is fearful and afraid, let him turn and depart at once from Mount Gilead.'* *"And twenty-two-thousand of the people returned, and ten thousand remained."* This strong mesmerizing fear leaves its victim terrified of life and circumstances. For the men in Gideon's army, fear became a hindrance to the Lord. God couldn't use them and sent them home. The

Preachers Outline and Sermon Bible explain what living in fear does to its victim. "Fear causes anxiety, dread, alarm, fright, panic, and terror. It causes all kinds of unpleasant emotions, phobias, neurosis, and even the more serious psychotic disorders. The torment of fear is one of the worst problems faced by man."

E – THE EVIL FEAR: 2 Timothy 1:7 *"For God has not given us a spirit of fear, but of power and of love and of a sound mind."* This kind of fear comes from the kingdom of darkness. This fear can impede everything you try to do. When the prince of darkness uses the *"Spirit of fear"* it robs God's people. The most important tools we have from the Lord are limited because of fear. Like LeBron James playing basketball with handcuffs, or Billy Graham at a crusade with duct tape on his mouth, are those who try to be a Christian and walk in fear. To excel in this life, it takes: the power of God, the Love of God, and the peace of God.

God's Side of Fear

A – THE APPROPRIATE FEAR: Deuteronomy 10:12 *"And now, Israel, what does the LORD your God require of you, but to fear the LORD your God, to walk in all His ways and to love Him, to serve the LORD your God with all your heart and with all your soul."* The right kind of fear means to be in awe of Almighty God. You respect the Father with all your heart and live according to His power, His love, and His ways. When you strive to please God and not disappoint Him, you are walking reverently. This suitable fear can keep you from sin (Ex. 20:20), which destroys.

R – THE REVERENT FEAR: Psalm 111:10 *"The fear of the LORD is the beginning of wisdom; A good understanding have all those who do His commandments."* According to the Bible, *"wisdom is the principal thing"* (Prov. 4:7). If wisdom were a giant room with all the information needed to live this life as God intended, the "fear of the Lord" would be the door. By the way, the huge room filled with all knowledge and information is your Bible (Deut. 4:6). The icing on the cake is; the Bible is Jesus Christ (John 1:1, 14; Rev. 19:13).

It's time to make a change and get off this road and lane. See "God's plan for you" at the back of this book.

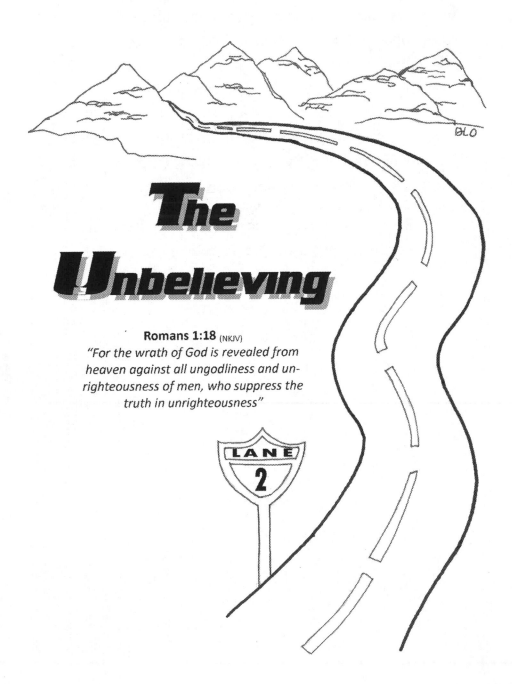

The Unbelieving

Romans 1:18 (NKJV)
"For the wrath of God is revealed from heaven against all ungodliness and un-righteousness of men, who suppress the truth in unrighteousness"

LANE
2

Lane Two – The UNBELIEVING

One day the world will admit the truth; that Jesus is the Son of God. Right now, most people don't believe that God sent His only Son to die for the sins of the world. Biblically, unbelief is a major problem. This lane consists of those who know of Jesus in their heads, but not in their hearts. For the hearts of many remain far from God (Matt. 15:8). What a person believes about Jesus Christ makes all the difference. One day Jesus asked His disciples, *"Who do men say that I, the Son of Man, am?"* (Matt. 16:13). During Jesus day, the masses thought he was John the Baptist, Elijah, Jeremiah or one of the other Old Testament prophets. Reading the story, we know that Peter by revelation of God said, *"You are the Christ, the Son of the living God"* (Matt. 16:16-17).

After Jesus died and rose again, a lie was propagated about Him. It was a matter of two reports; a good one and a bad one. The angels told the women that Jesus has risen and instructed them to *"Go quickly and tell His disciples that He is risen from the dead"* (Matt. 28:7). The lie and bad report was spread when the religious leaders bribed the guards, *"Tell them, 'His disciples came at night and stole Him away while we slept.' So they took the money and did as they were instructed; and this saying is commonly reported among the Jews until this day"* (Matt. 28:12-15). Today, the Jews still don't believe Jesus Christ was and is the Messiah, the Son of God. One day every unbeliever, in fact, every person who even lived will know the awesome power of Jesus' name. One day, *"Every knee should bow, of those in heaven, and of those on earth, and of those under the earth, and that every tongue should confess that Jesus Christ is Lord, to the glory of God the Father"* (Phil. 2:10-11).

Until that day, unbelief continues to wreak havoc in hearts and minds. We live in the information age; unbelief is a problem for Americans. According to a 2014 *The Truth Wins* article, "More Americans believe aliens have visited Earth than believe that Jesus is the Son of God." The article quotes a National Geographic survey that found that "77% of all Americans believe there are signs that aliens have visited earth." It also quoted a Harris poll which stated that "Only 68% of all Americans believe that Jesus is God or the Son of God." In America, because of secular schools, and secular homes, it is possible for a child to have never heard the name Jesus. Many of the people today don't really know who Jesus is. As in the first century Jesus is viewed as a mere prophet, a historical character, or just an ordinary person. Amazingly, some religions have him returning as a twisted diabolical person bent on killing and hurting those who don't follow their faith.

Don't be fooled, what we believe or don't believe about Jesus matters to God. Those who do not believe are in for a rude awakening. Those who do believe are saved and blessed. To believe in God's Son is much simpler than we know. It is within the grasp of everyone who hears the Word of God. The Bible is clear how a person can go from unbelief to belief. Salvation comes by grace through faith (Eph. 2:8-9). It is as simple as a thought going from the brain, through the heart (by faith) and out of the mouth (confession). Romans 10:8-11 states, *"The word is near you, in your mouth and in your heart" (that is, the word of faith which we preach): that if you confess with your mouth the Lord Jesus and believe in your heart that God has raised Him from the dead, you will be saved. For with the heart one believes unto righteousness, and with the mouth confession is made unto salvation. For the Scripture says, "Whoever believes on Him will not be put to shame."*

We live in a world where intellect has distorted the simple gospel message. Head knowledge has replaced heart knowledge.

When our actions, prove we know better than Almighty God, trouble is coming. Governments, schools, and businesses have evicted Biblical truths from society. The greater responsibility lies within the Christian home and the local church. Parents and pastors have not properly instructed their children about the simple truths of Christ. Our nation is becoming like the Jews in John chapter 8. They didn't believe that Jesus and the Father were one. This knowledge will cause a person to die a sinner (John 8:24). What is worse is the multitude of churches, and denominations that once believed in the Jesus found in scripture. They have ceased to follow God's established Word. This unbelief has made its way into the evangelical movement. There preachers and leaders dance around preaching on sin and even twist scriptures regarding who Jesus Christ

claimed to be. Unbelief has become a muddy trap; keeping its victims from moving forward and seeing the light. WE MUST WAKE UP TO THIS EVIL. The church in America has and will continue to pay a big price for being in and promoting this lane of unbelief.

When I ask Christians if they know people who once served the Lord, but no longer walk with Him; nearly every hand goes up. Why? It's because; the Christian community is struggling with unbelief and commitment. I'm not speaking of those going through a difficult season in their faith. I'm talking about those who, like a light cord have been pulled out of the power source; which is the Word of God. Their pursuit of God and the fruit of the Spirit are no longer evident. They have gone from belief and trust in God to unbelief and trust in self. Hebrews 3:12-14 says, *"Beware, brethren, lest there be in any of you an evil heart of unbelief in departing from the living God; but exhort one another daily, while it is called "Today," lest any of you be hardened through the deceitfulness of sin. For we have become partakers of Christ if we hold the beginning of our confidence steadfast to the end."*

The church, the people of God are falling away. While skeptics abound the hearts of unbelievers confirms that a time of apostasy is upon us. Paul also refers to *"Depart from the living God."* What does he mean? Let's be clear, the Apostle Paul is <u>not</u> speaking to unbelievers but to Christians? Paul not only uses the words, *"Beware brethren,"* but, to set up this chapter, Paul calls them *"Holy brethren, partakers of the heavenly calling"* (Heb. 3:1). Clearly, when the people of God have *"An evil heart of unbelief in departing from the faith"* this is cause for great concern. I believe this group is much larger than we realize.

Someone said, "Unbelief is the greatest sin." The Pew Research Center has reported that 2.4% of Americans identify themselves as atheists. An atheist is an unbeliever because he denies the existence of a deity. They are not alone. Even in Jesus' time, *"He did not do many mighty works there because of their unbelief"* (Matt. 13:58). Unbelief blinds people to the truth and robs them of hope and miracles. Like in Jesus' day, we the people failed to recognize Him as the Messiah. There are plenty of folks who walk in unbelief, denying that Jesus is the Son of God. What about the plethora of individuals who say they believe and follow Jesus, but their lifestyle and actions fall short of what they say.

Many believe "I'm basically a good person, so I'll go to heaven." Others believe, "God won't send me to hell because I don't live by the Bible." Still other believe, "Sure I do some bad things, but the really bad people like killers, and child molesters are the ones who go to hell." Are these people really true believers in Jesus? Do they trust in something other than Christ to save them? Still there are some who can't believe

> *The Great Apostasy*
>
> *The Apostle Paul warned that unbelief will cause some to "Depart from the faith"*

because they've never heard the truth about Jesus. Unbelief at any level is destructive, but is there a difference?

Biblically we can judge actions, which are also known as "Fruits" (Matt. 7:16). Determining the motives of the heart is God's business. The world has made the decision to lump all Christians into one category. On a plane I actually met a Muslim man who thought all American were Christians. In this book I separate Christians into three groups: true believers, Luke-warm believers, and fallen believers. I consider only the first group to be in right standing with God. As I already stated, the Bible is the final authority. It is the Word which sheds light on the true identity of the believer and unbeliever. Only God can know who is righteous and who is not. Again, the passage in Romans makes it clear, *"For with the heart one believes unto righteousness."* The Living Bible (TLB) uses the phrase *"Becomes right with God"* instead of the word *"righteousness."* If our belief is tied to righteousness, or being right with God, then 1 John 3:10 is vital to determining the difference between a true believer and an unbeliever. Like being hit right between the eyes, this verse says it all. *"Whoever does not practice righteousness is not of God"* (1 John 3:10). It would appear that practicing the faith is a key to being a true believer in Christ.

Earth is jam-packed with those who do not accept Jesus Christ as *"The only way to the Father"* (John 14:6). This single truth is not merely the elephant in the room. Instead, the truth about Jesus is the mastodon in every room. The world will one day deal with the issue of who Jesus Christ is. Right now, nations and states are getting away with unbelief. The terrible fact remains; too many don't believe the Bible's claim, which states accurately and unmistakably, the only way to heaven and eternal life comes through Jesus Christ. One of Satan's biggest lies has become a vestige of the many religions of the world. Without hesitation they promote many roads to heaven. Even our president said in the Chicago Times, "I believe there are many ways to heaven." This is alarming, especially when 57% of evangelicals believe as our president does. What matters most is the Bible. Take a Biblical journey with me and you see that the evidence is clear. There can be zero doubt that Jesus Christ is the ONLY WAY.

<u>Is Jesus Christ the ONLY way to heaven?</u>

- **We must go through Jesus the Word** (John 5:38-40) *"But you do not have His word abiding in you, because whom He sent, Him you do not believe. You search the Scriptures, for in them you think you have eternal life; and these are they which testify of Me. But you are not willing to come to Me that you may have life."*
- **We must believe in Jesus for everlasting life** (John 6:47) *"Most assuredly, I say to you, he who believes in Me has everlasting life."*

- **We must believe Jesus is God or we will dies in our sins** (John 8:24) *"Therefore I said to you that you will die in your sins; for if you do not believe that I am He, you will die in your sins."*

- **We must believe Jesus is the Savior of the World** (1 John 4:14) *"And we have seen and testify that the Father has sent the Son as Savior of the world."*

- **We must go through Jesus who is the door** (John 10:9) *"I am the door. If anyone enters by Me, he will be saved, and will go in and out and find pasture."*

- **We must believe Jesus is the Way** (John 14:6) *"Jesus said to him, 'I am the way, the truth, and the life. No one comes to the Father except through Me.'"*

- **We must be cleansed by the blood of Jesus** (Heb. 9:22) *"And according to the law almost all things are purified with blood, and without shedding of blood there is no remission."*

- **We must believe in the death, burial and resurrection of Jesus** (1 Cor. 15:1-4) *"Moreover, brethren, I declare to you the gospel which I preached to you, which also you received and in which you stand, by which also you are saved, if you hold fast that word which I preached to you--unless you believed in vain. For I delivered to you first of all that which I also received: that Christ died for our sins according to the Scriptures, and that He was buried, and that He rose again the third day according to the Scriptures."*

- **We must not preach anything other than Jesus** (Gal. 1:8-9) *"But even if we, or an angel from heaven, preach any other gospel to you than what we have preached to you, let him be accursed. As we have said before, so now I say again, if* *anyone preaches any other gospel to you than what you have received, let him be accursed."*

In Acts 4:12 Peter and John are defending Jesus to the Sanhedrin. This encounter was simply the beginning of the questions, harassment and eventual persecution these men of God would face. Like today, people were attempting to persuade them to stop using the name of Jesus. Soon, all the first century believers would face the same and even death because of Jesus. Yet, with the boldness of lions, Peter and John respond, *"Let it be known to you all, and to all the people of Israel, that by the name of Jesus Christ of Nazareth, whom you crucified, whom God raised from the dead...this is the 'stone which was rejected by you builders, which has become the chief cornerstone.' Nor is there salvation in any other, for there is no other name under heaven given among men by which we must be saved."* Notice the inimitable truth; you cannot be "saved" except by Jesus. They use the term *"By which we must be saved"* to emphasis their point. Where is our persuasion today?

With conviction, Dr. Jack Van Impe declares, "If you say there is any other way to heaven you are calling Christ a liar and a deceiver. Therefore, you cannot be saved." If he is right, imagine all those people walking around thinking they are saved, but in reality are lost. What are the ramifications to calling Jesus, who is the Word a lie? Could the true condition of the Body of Christ be worse off than we think? The true condition of the church is relative. By asking 10 different pastors or ministers, you'll have 10 different views on the condition of the Body of Christ. I believe the difference is stark. Like an artist and a regular person staring at the Mona Lisa; both appreciate the painting, but only one understands what he is looking at. Do you notice the increased unbelief around you? Do you see any cause to warn the people in your circle of influence?

Lane two has billions that move around freely and go on thinking they are safe and secure. Every day the masses wake up trusting in religion, good morals, or good works, to save their souls, instead of Jesus. I am truly disheartened. This lane is deceptive because believing isn't enough, for *"Even the demons believe and tremble"* (James 2:19), and are destined for hell (Matt. 25:41; Rev. 12:9). Believing in God isn't enough; your belief must take deeper root. *"Everyone that believes that Jesus is the Christ is born of God"* (1 John 5:1), and *"He who believes in Him is not condemned; but he who does not believe is condemned already, because he has not believed in the name of the only begotten Son of God"* (John 3:18). Belief must be rooted in the name of Jesus. The hustle and bustle of this lane of unbelief is solely for all who minimized or deny the Biblical Jesus.

This lane keeps people from seeing God's love through Jesus Christ. It tricks people into taking their head knowledge about two feet down the human body to the heart. Many in this lane are good people, heading for sudden ruin. As one minister put it, they are "In the path of the wrath of God. There is a hell, people are going there, and it lasts forever. And Jesus alone saves from sin. Jesus alone saves from death. Jesus alone saves from hell." A true believer is powerful and is exactly what God desires. One day Jesus said to the man who struggled with unbelief, *"If you can believe, all things are possible to him who believes"* (Mark 9:23). The man's response is an example to everyone on this lane. With tears in his eyes he said, *"Lord, I believe; help my unbelief!"* (Mark 9:24).

It's time to make a change and get off this road and lane.
See "God's plan for you" at the back of this book.

The Abominable

Proverbs 3:32 (NKJV)
"For the perverse person is an abomination to the LORD, But His secret counsel is with the upright."

LANE
3

Lane Three – The ABOMINABLE

My wife's favorite place is Disneyland. She loves everything about it; the atmosphere, main street, the stores, the themes, the characters, and of course the rides. Oh, and by the way, she really loves Tinkerbell too. There are several mountains in Disneyland such as, Space Mountain, Splash Mountain and Thunder Mountain. On one particular mountain is a beast called "The Abominable Snowman". As you jet through the Matterhorn Mountain ride, you will catch a glimpse of this ferocious creature. All along the downward journey, the beast can be seen and heard, bringing terror to children and adults alike.

Every time I hear the word "Abominable" I think of this "Mysterious creature with human or apelike characteristics reported to exist in the high Himalayas" (M-W.com). He is also known as "Yeti." Over the years, several have professed to have observed this killer frosty the snowman. The last known sighing was reported back in 2008.

Abominable is a word rarely used in our English language. It means, "Worthy of or causing disgust, quite disagreeable or unpleasant" (M-W.com). Synonyms are: abhorrent, offensive, appalling, awful, evil, foul, obscene, repulsive, and shocking. The Bible uses the word only 23 times in the King James Version, and 21 times in the New King James Version. The newer translations don't seem to like this word at all. I found 1 reference in the New International Version, 2 in the New Living Translation, and zero uses in the Holman Christian Standard Bible, God's Word, and New Century Version. Instead, these modern translations use words like: vile, detestable, immoral and degenerate. Abominable is a potent word God uses to describe very serious actions and attitudes. In Psalm 53:1 speaking about those who do abominable, corrupt things King David said, *"Their hearts are far from God."* Biblically, abominable sins are numerous, but nothing in our culture defines these deplorable sins better than homosexuality and sexual immorality. Lane's three and five on the broad road will cover these two categories in detail.

Let's be PERFECTLY CLEAR: God loves *"The whole world"* (John 3:16). Followers of Christ MUST love the people of the world as well. Anyone who doesn't love people as God does is in error. Jesus made this a commandment saying, *"A new commandment I give to you, that you love one another; as I have loved you, that you also love one another"* (John 13:34).

Let's be PERFECTLY CLREAR: True disciples and followers of Christ love one another (John 13:35). It's the misguided and spiritually immature who have hurt the Biblical message regarding homosexuality. The Bible says, *"Let all that you do be done with love"* (1 Cor. 16:14). That is the goal when dealing with sexual perversion and all serious sins. The spirit of love is powerful and can ease the tension between people.

In Jesus day, what was worse than a tax collector? Matthew was one. A tax collector was considered one of the most hated professions to the Jews. Therefore Matthew was hated by the establishment. Yet, Jesus saw his heart and potential, and called Matthew to leave that life and follow Him. There is hope for all of the people to turn from their sin and follow Christ. Jesus loved people, especially the lost, hurting and sinful. Matthew became a disciple and eventually wrote one of four Gospels. He settles the case regarding people when he wrote chapter 19. Quoting Jesus, Matthew said, *"You shall love your neighbor as yourself"* (Matt. 19:19). He goes even further quoting Jesus again, *"You shall love the Lord your God with all your heart, with all your soul, and with all your mind. This is the first and great commandment. And the second is like it: 'You shall love your neighbor as yourself.' On these two commandments hang all the Law and the Prophets"* (Matt. 22:37-40).

Again, let me be PERFECTLY CLEAR, I love people, all of them. Yet, just because I love the people on this highway, it doesn't mean I cannot speak out about how terribly wrong the homosexual lifestyle is. We must be able to effectively operate in love, hating the sin while loving the sinner, *"Pulling them out of the fire"* (Jude 1:21-23). This means following the golden rule: "Do unto others what you would have them do to you." God is serious about sin. It is because God loves, that He disciplines us. God created a standard by which He expects us to live by. When we fall short we miss out on His blessings and rewards. Ultimately, those who ignore His Word and His love, we will be judged.

Lane three, on the highway of evil, is for those who are naïve and live worldly lives. These people are corrupt in nature and love to touch and taste the impurities and lusts of the world. They have become stained, contaminated and polluted with worldliness. The homosexual lifestyle is abominable to God. They have exchanged natural affections for unnatural ones (Rom. 1:26-27). Therefore they have been *"Turned over to a reprobate (depraved) mind"* (Rom. 1:26-28).

This particular lifestyle is gaining more power in our culture. What God has condemned as evil the world embraces. What God has always punished is now becoming more and more acceptable in society. Even the new Pope, the leader of 1.1 billion people world-wide has "Indicated a change in tone, if not in teaching, in the church's stance toward gays and lesbians" (CNN.com). The secular progressive movement in our nation is working overtime to push this and other anti-biblical issues toward becoming acceptable in our society. They are winning for now. Alternative lifestyles, especially homosexuality have become the new revolution in America.

Currently 17 states have legalized gay marriage and more laws are being passed. Regardless of how scripture reads, or how states have voted, radical judges are by-passing it all. Those who flaunt the Homosexual agenda are winning. They are growing in popularity in our society. With radical judges, agenda driven law-makers and large voting-blocks, homosexuality is an accepted part of society. Sadly, those who live this way, and those who are fully accepting of this lifestyle have underestimate God's coming judgment. The further away from God and His standard we get, the sooner He will come and make things right. There is no doubt homosexuality and other abominable sins are having their day. This won't last.

Acceptance means rejecting God and His Word. With each passing law, America mocks the Living God. As each individual adheres to this unnatural way to love others, the sanctity of marriage is being destroyed. Mark my words, soon marriage will become a free-for-all institution. Given enough time, it will become legal to marry a dog, or a horse. Make no mistake about it, *"The wicked shall be turned into hell, And all the nations that forget God"* (Ps. 9:17).

The evidence is clear; America has forgotten its' God. There's an old saying, "When you mess with the bull, you get the horns." I find it interesting that the Bible used horns to point toward significant events in scripture. Beside animal horns and landmarks, there are two metaphorical uses of the word which I want to point out; one positive and one negative. First, Christ is called "A *horn of salvation for us"* (Luke 1:69), which The Holman Illustrated Bible Dictionary says is, "Signifying strength." The other horn is a series of judgments mentioned in the book of Revelation. These three sets of judgment are coming upon the *"Whole world"* (Luke 21:26). The second set is called the Trumpet Judgments. Revelation 8:2 says, *"I saw the seven angels who stand before God, and to them were given seven trumpets."* When these horns sound, the world will know the awesome power and judgment of God.

While sin is sin to the Father, all sin carries a different consequence. The sins in the category of "Abominable" are on a level all to themselves. When it comes to sin and judgment, man's opinion holds little weight, but what really matters is God's Word. Societies change, but God never does. Here is what God has always said about Abominations:

- **Leviticus 18:22** – *"You shall not lie with a male as with a woman. It is an <u>abomination</u>."*
- **Leviticus 20:13** – *"If a man lies with a male as he lies with a woman, both of them have committed an <u>abomination</u>. They shall surely be put to death. Their blood shall be upon them."*

- **Deuteronomy 22:5** – *"A woman shall not wear anything that pertains to a man, nor shall a man put on a woman's garment, for all who do so are an abomination to the Lord your God."*

- **Proverbs 6:16-19** – *"These six things the Lord hates, Yes, seven are an abomination to Him: A proud look, A lying tongue, Hands that shed innocent blood, A heart that devises wicked plans, Feet that are swift in running to evil, A false witness who speaks lies, And one who sows discord among brethren."*

- **Psalm 53:1-3** – *"The fool has said in his heart, "There is no God." They are corrupt, and have done abominable iniquity; there is none who does good. ^{2} God looks down from heaven upon the children of men, to see if there are any who understand, who seek God. ^{3} Every one of them has turned aside; they have together become corrupt; there is none who does good, No, not one."*

- **1 Corinthians 6:9** – *"Do you not know that the unrighteous will not inherit the kingdom of God? Do not be deceived. Neither fornicators, nor idolaters, nor adulterers, nor homosexuals, nor sodomites..."*

- **Romans 1:24-28** – *"Therefore God also gave them up to uncleanness, in the lusts of their hearts, to dishonor their bodies among themselves, who exchanged the truth of God for the lie, and worshiped and served the creature rather than the Creator, who is blessed forever. Amen. For this reason God gave them up to vile passions. For even their women exchanged the natural use for what is against nature. Likewise also the men, leaving the natural use of the woman, burned in their lust for one another, men with men* committing what is shameful, and receiving in themselves the penalty of their error which was due. And even as they did not like to retain God in their knowledge, God gave them over to a debased mind, to do those things which are not fitting..."

- **Titus 1:16** – "They profess to know God, but in works they deny Him, being <u>abominable</u>, disobedient, and disqualified for every good work."
- **1 Peter 4:3** – "For we have spent enough of our past lifetime in doing the will of the Gentiles—when we walked in lewdness, lusts, drunkenness, revelries, drinking parties, and <u>abominable</u> idolatries."

It's time to make a change and get off this road and lane. See "God's plan for you" at the back of this book.

The Murderers

Psalm 37:32 (NKJV)
*"The wicked watches the righteous,
And seeks to slay him."*

LANE
4

Lane Four – The MURDERERS

The travelers of this lane are easy to spot. These people have blood on their hands, and evil in their hearts, for they have *"Shed innocent blood"* (Prov. 6:17). These belong to a despicable group which *"The Lord hates"* (Prov. 6:16). What a horrible place to be, one who is hated by the Father. The New International Version (NIV) says, *"It is a dreadful thing to fall into the hands of the living God"* (Heb. 10:31). Murderers are selfish and will get what they deserve, as we all will. Murderers, assassins, slayers of the innocent, butchers, and executioners take life into their own hands. They take what is precious to God (Eph. 2:10) and terminate it in moments of rage; and even worse, in calculated plotting and scheming.

God gave man dominion over the fish of the sea, the animals and the earth itself (Gen. 1:26). He made human beings in His own image, putting His blessing on us and gave us a very important mandate, *"Be fruitful and multiply; fill the earth and subdue it; have dominion over the fish of the sea, over the birds of the air, and over every living thing that moves on the earth"* (Gen. 1:28). Instead of leading and inspiring people, murderers have selfishly lived to destroy individuals, families and even millions of people. Murderers waste the *"Breath of life"* (Gen. 2:7) that God has given His creation. Murderers even rob Americans of their right to *"Life, liberty, and the Pursuit of happiness"* located in the opening sentence of the Declaration of Independence. Many, with one stroke of a pen, have massacred millions. Kings, Presidents and leaders, with one command have taken away life. Today, taking a life has become as easy as taking candy from a baby. Some conspirators, never pull the trigger themselves, but have the ability to convince and send others to do the job.

Murder statistics are always alarming. According to the Federal Bureau of Investigation the murder rate in the U.S. was 14,827 in 2013. The city of Chicago won the honors for "Murder city USA" with 412 murders. I can only imagine what our Creator thinks? Biblically, murderers don't fair very well in the end. God's judgment should be a scary thought for all ponderers of slaughter. Like all sin, selfishness is at the

root. Those who take innocent lives think about themselves and no one else. Murder comes in a variety of ways. Only God understands the total scope of life and death. He has a plan for those who give life and take it. Dietrich Bonhoeffer said, *"God has reserved to Himself the right to determine the end of life, because He alone knows the goal to which it is His will to lead it. It is for Him alone to justify a life or to cast it away."*

When considering murder there is one topic that half the country would like to leave out of the equation, and that is abortion. Abortion, which is a selfish act, legally took root on January 22, 1973, *Row vs. Wade*. When it became the law of the land, I believe America's days were numbered. This topic alone is responsible for much debate and still divides our nation. When I told my wife Michele I was writing this section, she said to me, "It wasn't the day they legalized abortions, it was the day they legalized murder." The very day I was penning this part of the book, and looked up the date the law took effect; it was also January 22nd, but 41 years later. Interesting!

The country is divided into two groups; the "Pro-Life" crowd, and the "Pro-Choice" crowd. Amazingly, not all religious people, especially those who claim to adhere to the Holy Scriptures are Pro-Lifers. I admit this perplexes me greatly and is further proof believers have been deceived and accept the lies told them. In my small town I have witnessed pastor's struggle with this issue and a few change their stance. Whether or not the life growing inside the mother's womb is called a baby or a fetus, an abortion ends the pregnancy and destroys what was living. The beating heart, the flowing blood, the dividing cells, and the process which end at birth are stopped short. We can all agree an abortion ends a pregnancy. Pregnancy is defined: (1) The Merriam-Webster dictionary says it is, *"The condition of a woman or female animal that is going to have a baby or babies"* (2) The American Heritage Stedman's Medical Dictionary defines it as *"The period from conception to birth."* After the egg is fertilized by a sperm, cell division begins, by mitosis and meiosis. By the way, according the Bible, the sperm is, *"A man's seed"* (Lev. 15:16). As the development continues many amazing things happen. By the end of the first month the heart starts to beat and pump blood. About 40 weeks later a baby is born.

Every year, staggeringly millions of abortions are carried out around the world. Darris McNeely in her article *The Abortion Debate: What does God Say* said, "Each day about 120,000 lives—enough to populate a medium-sized city—are terminated by abortion, a practice legal in most countries. But how does God view the taking of the lives of millions of the unborn—or even one, for that matter?"

In light of the conversations God had with Job, Moses, Jeremiah, the Psalmist and others in scripture, it is quite a stretch for the proponents of *choice* to call the child growing in the mother's womb a fetus or worse; a piece of a woman's tissue. Our foundation and source, which is the Word of God, tells us it is a living child being formed and planned by Almighty God. THIS IS THE BIBLICAL TRUTH. Skeptics, doubter and deniers will probably never see the truth. Those still open to the Gospel, which is the truth (John 17:17), need to see the Father's heart. Unfortunately, eyes are blinded to the truth because of the spirit of deception at work in the world.

The Bible isn't fuzzy on the subject of abortion, like some contend. In reality, it speaks openly and precisely about what is living inside the womb. The Bible, especially, Matthew 1:18, Exodus 21:22-23, and Genesis 25:21-22, settles the case. More than being "Pro-Life" or "Pro-choice" we as believing Christian's should be "PRO-BIBLE" because there is wavering on the truth; which sets us free (John 8:32). The Heavenly Father has a lot to say about this divisive topic.

- **Genesis 25:21-23** – *"Now Isaac pleaded with the Lord for his wife, because she was barren; and the Lord granted his plea, and Rebekah his wife conceived. But the children struggled together within her; and she said, "If all is well, why am I like this?" So she went to inquire of the Lord. And the Lord said to her: "Two nations are in your womb, two peoples shall be separated from your body; one people shall be stronger than the other, And the older shall serve the younger."*
- **Exodus 20:13** – *"You shall not murder."*

- **Exodus 21:22-23** – *"If men fight, and hurt a woman with child, so that she gives birth prematurely, yet no harm follows, he shall surely be punished accordingly as the woman's husband imposes on him; and he shall pay as the judges determine. But if any harm follows, then you shall give life for life..."*
- **Jeremiah 1:4-5** – *"Then the word of the Lord came to me, saying: 'Before I formed you in the womb I knew you; before you were born I sanctified you.'"*
- **Job 3:3** – *"A male child is conceived."*
- **Job 3:16** – *"Why was I not hidden like a stillborn child, like infants who never saw light?"*
- **Job 31:15** – *"Did not He who made me in the womb make them? Did not the same One fashion us in the womb?"*
- **Psalm 127:3-5** – *"Behold, children are a heritage from the Lord, The fruit of the womb is a reward."*
- **Psalm 139:13-14** – *"For You formed my inward parts; You covered me in my mother's womb. I will praise You, for I am fearfully and wonderfully made."*
- **Matthew 1:18** – *"Now the birth of Jesus Christ was as follows: After His mother Mary was betrothed to Joseph, before they came together, she was found with child of the Holy Spirit."*
- **Matthew 1:20** – *"But while he thought about these things, behold, an angel of the Lord appeared to him in a dream, saying, "Joseph, son of David, do not be afraid to take to you Mary your wife, for that which is conceived in her is of the Holy Spirit."*
- **Matthew 1:22-23** – *"So all this was done that it might be fulfilled which was spoken by the Lord through the prophet, saying: "Behold, the virgin shall be with child, and bear a Son,*

and they shall call His name Immanuel," which is translated, "God with us."

- **Luke 20:38** – "For He is not the God of the dead but of the living, for all live to Him."

Think about it, Mary wasn't instantly nine months pregnant when "She was found with child of the Holy Spirit (Matt. 1:18). Something powerful had happened to her, like in Acts 19:6 when the "Holy Spirit came upon them, and they spoke with tongues and prophesied." In an instant, Mary was pregnant and the process of cell division begun in her body. Like all humans, Jesus began as one tiny cell, when life begins. Thus, the process to bringing Jesus Christ as the Savior into the world was initiated. In this case, the Holy Spirit by-passed the man's seed, anointing one of Mary's eggs, "For that which is conceived in her is of the Holy Spirit" (Matt. 1:20). Jesus would be both the "Son of God" (John 10:36), and the "Son of man" (Luke 6:5), He had to go through the same process as all human beings do in order to be delivered. So, when "The days were completed for her to be delivered" (Luke 2:6), Jesus was born. Like in all pregnant women this was around 40 weeks.

According to God's perfect design, life begins at conception. The Holy Spirit came upon Mary when she was without child. God didn't wait until Jesus was born to touch him. He decided to work within the same process that all mankind does, the human gestation. God is all-powerful. He could have zapped Jesus down to earth as a 30 year old man to begin His work. This wasn't His plan for God's seed, not man's seed was paramount. Jesus would need to identify with us, by "Taking the form of a bondservant, and coming in the likeness of men. And being found in appearance as a man, He humbled Himself and became obedient to the point of *death, even the death of the cross"* (Phil. 2:7-8). Fact is, God's seed is the Word (Luke 8:11), and the Word is Jesus Christ (John 1:1, 14). Don't be deceived any longer. Wake up to the truth of God's Word. The Holy Spirit, like a man's seed initiated the spark for life to begin in Mary the mother of Jesus.

Let's be crystal clear, abortion is murder. Thankfully God forgives murder and all sins (Matt. 12:31). I believe that abortion is a biblical issue. First, the shedding of innocent blood is murder (Gen. 4:10; Prov. 6:16-19). Second, in God's eyes, the unborn child is precious; not a piece of tissue (Jer. 1:5). Abortion is wrong on several other levels. Like all sin, it is rooted in human selfishness. For the most part, babies are destroyed for convenience sake. Some may not realize it, but abortion is also an end-times issue. In fact, murder and selfishness are staple issues during the times before the end. The Bible is based on servant-hood (Matt. 20:25-27), self-sacrifice (Rom. 12:1), loving one-another (John 13:34), humility (Phil. 2:3), and self-denial (Mark 8:34). People in general, but women in this case, are programed with the mantra, "It's my body, I have the right to choose." That's exactly what a murderer would say. When life becomes focused on convenience and personal human rights over what is noble and right, trouble is mounting. Mother Teresa said, *"It is a poverty to decide that a child must die so that you may live as you wish."*

> *"Christ died that we might live. This is the opposite of abortion. Abortion kills that someone might live differently" -John Piper*

Now, let me speak to all women who call themselves believers. With much fear and trembling I want to paint a different picture than what the culture has painted regarding women and their bodies. There are two groups of Christian women, those who are married to a man and those who are married to Christ. Actually, all of us, both men and women are married to Christ. The Bible informs us that the church is the bride of Christ (2 Cor. 11:2). The secular culture continues to divide us, creating a greater distance between the laws of the land and the Word of God. As believers, discarding the authority of the written Word is detrimental to understanding the role of women in the country. Some in our country want us to believe there is a war on women. The only war on women is Satan's attempts to deceive. His plan is to alter God's Word and change who and what women in our culture are supposed to be. When women realize *"Charm is deceitful and beauty is passing"* (Prov. 31:30), and *"Strength and honor are her clothing"* (Prov. 31:25), they will truly shine. Understanding their very high calling in God's Kingdom, will unleash everything God intended them to be. Maybe then, abortion and other lies about women will diminish.

Remember, God chose a simple, humble girl from Nazareth to mother the Son of God. When the angel appeared he said, *"Rejoice, highly favored one, the Lord is with you; blessed are you among women!"* (Luke 1:28). Not only was Mary chosen and honored, but *women* in general were chosen as well. For, *"Children are a heritage from the Lord, The fruit of the womb is a reward"* (Ps. 127:3). Without a doubt a Proverbs 31 women is highly respected by the Lord. Verse 30 goes on to say, *"A woman who fears the Lord, she shall be praised."*

Not long ago the Lord showed me this progression of four verses. I hope it will shed some light on the abortion issue and steer women, men and believers toward the loving Father and His awesome Word. The Word of God declares:

- **Your body is the temple of the Holy Spirit.** In other words, what you do with it matters to God. THE WORD OF GOD DECLARES in **1 Corinthians 6:19** – *"Do you not know that your body is the temple of the Holy Spirit who is in you, whom you have from God, and you are not your own?"*

- **Your body is not yours alone.** Society and the culture has told you that you are free to bare it, flaunt it, abuse it, and even kill the life in it. Margaret Sanger, the founder of Planned Parenthood said, "No woman can call herself free who does not control her own body." This is wrong. This is a lie from the pit of hell. This is NOT biblical. If you are married your body not only belongs to you, but also to your husband. And if you are single, you and your body belong to Christ. THE WORD OF GOD DECLARES in **1 Corinthians 7:4** – *"The wife does not have authority over her own body, but the husband does. And likewise the husband does not have authority over his own body, but the wife does."*

- As a believer in Jesus Christ, **you are a part of the Body of Christ**. He is the head of the church and people gathered in churches make up His body. What we do with the Body of Christ is valued in the kingdom of God. THE WORD OF GOD DECLARES in **1 Corinthians 12:27** – *"Now you are the body of Christ, and members individually"* (Col. 1:18; Rom. 12:5).

- **You and your body were created for God's purpose.** Someone said, *"God doesn't make junk."* Never forget, *"You are fearfully and wonderfully made"* (Ps. 139:14). Every unborn child is precious to God. This includes the blind, deformed, and disabled. What man has labeled a problem, an inconvenience, a piece of tissue, God has called wonderful. THE WORD OF GOD DECLARES in **Romans**

12:1-2 – "I beseech you therefore, brethren, by the mercies of God, that you present your bodies a living sacrifice, holy, acceptable to God, which is your reasonable service. And do not be conformed to this world, but be transformed by the renewing of your mind, that you may prove what is that good and acceptable and perfect will of God."

In our great nation, many voices can be heard regarding abortion. Make no mistake; the only clear, balanced and authoritative voice is the Word of God. God's plan is a loving relationship with us, not some political viewpoint. The proponents of abortion are liars, deceivers and murderers. Whoever coined the phrase, *"The womb is the most dangerous place in world"* was right. Not only is abortion dangerous, it is one of Satan's greatest tools to destroy God's people before they even take their first breath of life. Taking a closer look reveals that Planned Parent began as a way to eliminate blacks from society. Even Pastor Clenard Childress Jr. said, "The most dangerous place for an African-American is in the womb." The truth, which will never become a main stream news report, would change many hearts and minds. An open and honest look at this topic is enlightening. Studying this topic in depth would do everyone some good.

According to BlackGenocide.com, founded by Clenard Childress Jr., "Planned Parenthood is the largest abortion provider in America? 78% of their clinics are in minority communities. Blacks make up 12% of the population, but 35% of the abortions in America. Are we being targeted? Isn't that genocide? We are the only minority in America that is on the decline in population. If the current trend continues, by 2038 the black vote will be insignificant. Did you know that the founder of Planned

Parenthood, Margaret Sanger, was a devout racist who created the Negro Project designed to sterilize unknowing black women and others she deemed as undesirables of society? The founder of Planned Parenthood said, "Colored people are like human weeds and are to be exterminated."

This lane is messy and bloody. We as believers have failed to address this issue; it has morphed into greater problems. According to the *Daily Caller*, "In May 2013 Dr. Kermit Gosnell was convicted on three murder charges and 21 felony counts of illegal late-term abortions, among other charges. He is currently serving a life sentence."

If we don't stand in the gap for the unborn, more people will suffer. Abortion is an end-times *"Doctrine of demons"* (1 Tim. 4:1), with a specific strategy to confuse and destroy God's people. Remember, there is only one truth, God's Word. In John 8 Jesus explained who Satan is; a liar and a murder. He said, *"Why do you not understand My speech? Because you are not able to listen to My word. You are of your father the devil, and the desires of your father you want to do. He was a murderer from the beginning, and does not stand in the truth, because there is no truth in him. When he speaks a lie, he speaks from his own resources, for he is a liar and the father of it"* (John 8:43-44). America has sanitized abortion of murder and has legitimized it. Abortion is an act of murder. All willing parties are guilty and need to repent. Satan has lied and deceived over half of all Americans into believing that abortion is okay because it is the law of the land. It may be legal, but it doesn't mean that it is right in God's eyes. The next time you hear a commentator spouting on about this issue, sync up his or her words with scripture. The Bible stands forever against this hideous sin. Regardless of the facts and what God says, the supporters of abortion, Christians and non-Christians are self-seeking, confused and blind to the truth. Line up their agenda with God's and realize the difference.

God's desire is that we walk with Him. Abortion is not only murder and sin, but it goes against God's will for mankind. There's a story about a man in the Bible who interrupted God's plan for procreation and the family. Within the Mosaic Law, the Law of the Leverite (Deut. 25:5) required Onan to marry his brother's widow Tamar; to raise offspring for his brother who died. Onan's refusal to do the right thing caused God to deal severely with him. The Amplified (AMP) in Genesis 38:9-10 says, *"Onan knew that the family would not be his, so when he cohabited with his brother's widow, he prevented conception, lest he should raise up a child for his brother. And the thing which he did displeased the Lord; therefore He slew him also."* In fact, Onan's story is part and parcel the basis for the Catholic Churches doctrine on birth control and contraception.

> *Abortion interrupts God's plan for mankind*

We are created to love and give life, not take it. Our lives should be spent loving and protecting one another. We are considered the temple God. In 2 Corinthians 6:18 declares, *"You are the temple of the living God. I will dwell in them And walk among them. I will be their God, And they shall be My people. Therefore Come out from among them And be separate, says the Lord. Do not touch what is unclean, And I will receive you. I will be a Father to you, And you shall be My sons and daughters, Says the Lord Almighty."* Due to being aborted, how many millions were denied the opportunity to be a child of God?

Americans have not done enough, with the end goal of eradicating abortion, while the church community has lost its fortitude and power. Only Almighty God can step in now. Tragically, this lane on the road to Gehenna, the lake of fire, has been allowed to expand. The Bible is clear about the murderers who live in the fourth lane, *"Whoever sheds man's blood, by man his blood shall be shed; for in the image of God He made man"* (Gen. 9:6).

It's time to make a change and get off this road and lane.
See "God's plan for you" at the back of this book.

The Sexually Immoral

1 Corinthians 6:18 (NKJV)
"Flee sexual immorality. Every sin that a man does is outside the body, but he who commits sexual immorality sins against his own body."

LANE
5

Lane Five – The WHOREMONGER AND IMMORAL

Going overseas is life-changing. Coming back with a new appreciation for America is certain. Most people in the world are not afforded the three basic rights the Declaration of Independence guarantees each of its citizens, *"Life, liberty and the pursuit of happiness."*

Things have changed since the second Congregational Congress met on that faithful day on July 4, 1776. In my short lifetime, I have witnessed the deterioration of our country moral compass. Our nation has compromised the moral foundation it has stood on for over 200 years. The founders paid the ultimate price, their lives, to establish a moral and upright nation under God. Our founders included the phrase "unalienable rights" which the Declaration says all human beings have been given by their Creator. "Over 200 years ago they shook off the chains of tyranny from Great Britain, by divine call. Citing 27 biblical violations they wrote the Declaration of Independence with liberty and justice for all. But something happened since Jefferson called the Bible the cornerstone for American liberty then put it in our schools as a light. Or since 'Give me liberty, or give me death,' Patrick Henry said. Our country was founded on the Gospel of Jesus Christ. We eliminated God from the equation of American life, thus eliminating the reason this nation first began" (America Again by Carman).

In Matthew 24:32 Jesus prophetically describes Israel as a fig tree. If America were a tree the immoral on this road would be the lumberjacks swinging and chopping away at its base. One day America the great will be felled and cut down by our own immorality. When immorality rises, nations eventually fall. Kerby Anderson in his article *When Nations Die* says, "When the traditional beliefs of a nation erode, the nation dies. Religion provides the set of standards that govern a nation." History shows that nations come and go. When a nation dies you can bet it was knee deep in immorality; which Greece and Rome are prime examples. The Historian Will Durant said, "There is no significant example in history, before our time, of a society successfully maintaining moral life without the aid of religion."

I've been to India and Uganda twice. The people in India and Africa were some of the most gracious, caring and beautiful people. So far, nothing in my life compares to walking down the streets and villages in these nations. Seeing the love of God on the faces of people in a foreign land was awesome. Plus, watching the fire of God at work on the other side of the world was eye-opening. Spending time in their homes, communities and churches was unforgettable. Compared to America, they had nothing.

Then, I saw the Jesus in them and realized they had everything. I saw their love for one another despite their overwhelming needs. I saw their passion and hunger for Christ, and was touched.   In Hyderabad, India I couldn't walk down beautiful streets. I didn't see manicured lawns, or street sweepers coming down the block. In disbelief I traveled through neighborhoods, and everything was chaotic, dirty and unsanitary. I thought to myself, didn't they care? People filled the streets, dirt and trash where everywhere. The most heart wrenching was the villages. Off the beaten path, poverty stricken, filled with hundreds of people living in simple huts and homes. What I saw with the natural eye in India and Africa reminded me of the spiritual condition I see in America.

Open sewers was the most awful thing; little trenches coming from each house and running down uneven dirt streets. In one particular Indian village, they shared one outhouse. It was completely unusable. So, how did the people use the bathroom? I was shocked by the experience one of the women on our team had. When nature called, the pastor's wife took her into their home. It was a simple house with three rooms. She was taken into the furthest room, the kitchen area. What happened next was jaw-dropping. She was told to go to the bathroom on the floor. I cannot imagine doing this? Each house had a small hole in the corner in the back room. A bucket of water was used to wash the waste through the hole in the corner and out of the house. A small open ditch would drain into another and the waste was carried away to who knows where. This and worse is life for millions of people around the world. Imagine stepping over a ditch full of bodily waste each time you walk into the front door of your home.

It was more of the same in Africa. I visited one of the slums where thousands of Ugandans live. I watched innocent children playing barefoot and shirtless in the trash heap they call their backyard. In shock and tears I watched many of them happily and joyfully run, jump and play. They seemed unaware they were living in the middle of filth. For them, it was all they knew. This too reminds me of my own country.

America is suffering from the same fate, but with a twist. We laugh, play, buy and sell unaware that our immorality is killing us from the inside out. Hidden behind the groomed sidewalks, shady parks, and lavish homes is a filth that is permeating our land. The stench isn't obvious, like the open sewers in India or the slums of Uganda. As each lumberjack of immorality lands blow after blow, only the spiritual can see it for what it is. We have gone from a Biblically moral based nation to a secular nation, and immorality turning us into a godless nation.

Even the Founder's knew about immorality, which is something they warned us about. "Of the 55 men who formed the Constitution 52 were active members of their church. Founding fathers like Noah Webster who wrote the first dictionary could literally quote the Bible chapter and verse. James Madison said, 'We've staked our future on our ability to follow the Ten Commandments with all our heart.' These men believed you couldn't even call yourself an American if you subvert the Word of God. In his farewell address, Washington said, 'You can't have national morality apart from religious principle,' and it's true 'cause right now we have nearly 150,000 kids carrying guns to these war zones we call public schools. In the '40's and '50's student problems were chewing gum and talking. In the '90's, rape and murder are the trend. The only way this nation can even hope to last this decade is put God in America again" (America Again by Carman).

America has serious problems; debt, terrorism and political division to name a few. We are split down the middle of several key issues. Our greater problem is spiritual in nature. Most Americans are unaware of the spiritual giants in the land. Ephesians 5:5-6 in the Holman Christian Standard Bible says, *"Know and recognize this: no sexually immoral or impure or greedy person, who is an idolater, has an inheritance in the kingdom of the Messiah and of God. Let no one deceive you with empty arguments, for because of these things God's wrath is coming on the disobedient."* America's leaders have failed to recognize the outcome immorality is having on us. Bradford G. Schleifer in his article *The Immorality Explosion* said, "Old-style morality is under assault like never before. Many have come to wonder what is right and what is wrong—what morality really is. A new perverse subculture has crept into nearly every home and every society." This is nothing new, the Apostle Paul made sure the church understood *"Not to keep company with sexually immoral people"* (1 Cor. 5:9). Imagine if the 1960's, free-love crowd, who by their lifestyle embraced immorality, didn't get their way. On the other hand, imagine if believers in Christ would have put their foot down; refusing to allow immorality to come flooding onto the scene. Things would be drastically different. The trend continues because many are failing to stand up for God's Word; which is escalating. It's difficult to live godly in the midst of the upsurge of immorality and sin. I am weary with the rising tide of believers who are falling down because of sexual sins. Jack Frost in *Ministry Today* said, "There is an alarming trend of moral failure among leaders. There is an epidemic of moral failure in church leadership today." *Focus on the Family* did a study that reported "We in the United States lose a pastor a day because he seeks an immoral path instead of God's." Let me share some shocking statistics with you.

- Sex is the #1 thing people search for on the internet (TopTenReviews).
- Every 39 minutes a new pornographic video is created in the United States (TopTenReviews).

- 7 of 10 lay leaders in the church admitted to visiting adult web-sites at least once a week. 5 of 10 pastors said they did the same (thealabamabaptist.org).
- 12 to 17 year olds are the largest consumers of internet pornography (TopTenReviews).
- 50% of all Christian men and 20% of all Christian women are addicted to pornography (ChristiaNet.org).

"Abe Lincoln said, 'The philosophy of the classroom in one generation will be the philosophy of government of the next.' So when you eliminate the Word of God from the classroom and politics you eliminate the nation that Word protects. America is now number one in teen pregnancy and violent crime. America is number one in illiteracy, drug use, and divorce. Everyday a new holocaust of 5,000 unborn die, while pornography floods our streets like open sewers. America's dead and dying hand is on the threshold of the Church, while the spirit of Sodom and Gomorrah vex us all. When it gets to the point where people would rather come out of the closet than clean it, it's a sign that the judgment of God is gonna fall" (America Again by Carman).

I believe God is longsuffering, waiting for our hearts to change. Of course, He knows if and when we will. Just as *"God so loved the world that He gave is only Son"* (John 3:16), God's so loved the world that He is giving us time to repent. If we don't clean up our act, God will indeed bring action. It's a matter of walking in the spirit or walking in our own lusts. Galatians 5:16-21 teaches us the difference:

"I say then: Walk in the Spirit, and you shall not fulfill the lust of the flesh. For the flesh lusts against the Spirit, and the Spirit against the flesh; and these are contrary to one another, so that you do not do the things that you wish.

But if you are led by the Spirit, you are not under the law. Now the works of the flesh are evident, which are: adultery, fornication, uncleanness, lewdness, idolatry, sorcery, hatred, contentions, jealousies, outbursts of wrath, selfish ambitions, dissensions, heresies, envy, murders, drunkenness, revelries, and the like; of which I tell you beforehand, just as I also told you in time past, that those who practice such things will not inherit the kingdom of God."

When you walk in the spirit you will demonstrate the fruit of the spirit. The fruit of the Spirit is love, joy, peace, longsuffering, kindness, goodness, faithfulness, gentleness, self-control. Against such there is no law. And those who are Christ's have crucified the flesh with its passions and desires. If we live in the Spirit, let us also walk in the Spirit. Because more and more in America and in the church are pursuing their godless passions and desires, the moral code in the land is changing.

The whole definition and view of sex has changed in our culture. Not long ago any kind of interaction between two people was defined "a sex act." It was Jesus who said, "*Whoever looks at a woman to lust for her has already committed adultery with her in his heart*" (Matt. 5:28). According to the Savior we have debased His standard. The battle field is the mind. Consider the Monica Lewinsky political sex scandal in 1998. Remember our sitting president, Bill Clinton? On national television he redefined the activity between himself and Monica Lewinsky (an employee), which transpired inside the oval office. He declared his actions were, "not sex." When the highest leader of our land, the most powerful man on earth, minimizes what the Bible calls adultery, God's wrath is sure to come. Is the *"Cup of God indignation"* (Rev. 14:10) ready to be poured out upon the wickedness of our nation?

A recent survey by the Barna Group asked adults which, if any, of eight behaviors with moral overtones they had engaged in during the past week. The behaviors included looking at pornography (19%), using profanity (28%), gambling (20%), gossiping (12%), engaging in sexual intercourse with someone to whom they were not married (9%), retaliating against someone (8%), getting drunk (12%), and lying (11%). One of the shocking things this survey indicated is that younger generations are two times more likely to engage in immoral behaviors; including nine times more likely to engage in sex outside of marriage, and two times more likely to view pornography.

Today, we have an immorality eruption. Like a volcano slowly building up pressure, sexual immorality has reached an all-time high. The molten lava of destruction, once hidden and buried is oozing down the mountain, filling hearts and homes with perversion. This wickedness has turned powerful men and nations into nothingness. It's sad to admit, but America's sin is catching up to her. Soon the Lord will step in and judgment will began.

The whoremonger and sexually immoral strive to rule the day. The eruption, which began in the 60's, has become a death cloud. Now, with the birth of the internet, the death cloud of dust has opened endless possibilities for sexual sin. This pyroclastic flow has reached the atmosphere spreading its evil demise around the world. With one click of a button, innocent eyes are being opened. Nothing good comes from this kind of sin. Like the fruit in the garden of Eden, God is warning this generation, not to partake nor even touch the wickedness on this road *"lest you die"* (Gen. 3:3).

The problem is a spiritual one. Its demonic hold is growing and reaching younger victims. This is not just an adult problem anymore. Our children are exposed to every kind of perversion; from nude pictures to forums discussing "same-sex relationships." Younger and younger our children are being robbed of their innocence; forced to grow up. Just as their eyes were open in the Garden of Eden, our children are forced to experience evil too soon. According to Real Truth Magazine, "In today's world, it is common to lose one's virginity by age 16."

Satan is working his magic, watching our "tolerate society" promote re-educating our kids. Right out of the gate, Satan is feeding off of our lust and weaknesses. He is benefiting from our poor choices and vices. In the book *Adultery the Forgivable Sin* there are some statistics: (1) 80% of marriages will suffer some form of adultery and often end in divorce. (2) 50% of marriages end in divorce. (3) 66% of second marriages end in divorce. (4) 70% of third marriages end in divorce. (5) Only 35% of marriages survive an affair.

All believers should know, "God hates divorce" (Mal. 2:16). All believes should know that we are doomed without a moral compass. The world will pursue immorality to satisfy its lusts, but the Body of Christ must not. Yet, many are trapped because of bad choices. Has the local church lost its way? We cannot serve God and immoral desires. Believers have the Word of God as a light and are without excuse (Rom. 1:20). We are witnessing our nation change from a moral country to an immoral one. Without the Bible, we are doomed. Samuel Adams in a letter to John Trumbull said, "Religion and good morals are the only solid foundation of public liberty and happiness."

So, what is a whoremonger? Dictionary.com says, "Someone who consorts with whores; a lecher or pander." A panderer is a person who furnishes clients for a prostitute or supplies persons for illicit sexual intercourse; procurer; pimp, a person who caters to or profits from the weaknesses or vices of others. According to Yourdefinition.com, "A whoremonger is a customer of a prostitute." Several definitions make reference to "Pimp," which is a procurer of whores." Long ago, God warned us of this coming immoral lifestyle. We have become sexually impure; those who commit fornication; sex before marriage, and adultery. It was only a matter of time until our sexual immorality would become abominations. Homosexuality and other sexual acts which God forbids are promoted in our nation.

America's infatuation with this lane is obvious, as well as the eventual righteous judgment of God. People have become *"Filled with all unrighteousness, sexual immorality, wickedness, covetousness, maliciousness; full of envy, murder, strife, deceit, evil-mindedness; they are whisperers, backbiters, haters of God, violent, proud, boasters, inventors of evil things, disobedient to parents, undiscerning, untrustworthy, unloving, unforgiving, unmerciful; who, knowing the righteous judgment of God, that those who practice such things are deserving of death, not only do the same but also approve of those who practice them"* (Rom. 1:29-32).

Again, where does the Body of Christ fit into this mess? Have we taken the twenty-three ungodly actions mentioned in the verses above and embraced them as our own? In John 7:38 Jesus mentions *"Rivers of living water"* flowing out of those who believe. When the Body of Christ continues to embrace the garbage of the world, we pollute that river and make it harder for others to know  Christ. The actions of the Body of Christ today are being witnessed by those living downstream. Our love for garbage rather than our passion for Christ are now slowly floating down the river. Maybe it's time for a river cleansing ceremony.

We are living in the last hours, and the warning goes out to awaken the church, and warn those living large on the 8-Lane Highway. A clear sign we are living in the last days is the increased spirit of lust. The world is bragging about immorality, while the Christian community struggles with it. The pews of the church are beginning to stink from this kind of living. Sadly, the church is becoming more like the world instead of more like Jesus. 1 John 2:15-18 warns against unfaithfulness and worldliness.

- **It is the last hour** – *"Little children, it is the last hour..."* (Vs. 18).
- **You cannot have it both ways - love God or love the world** – *"Do not love the world or the things in the world. If anyone loves the world, the love of the Father is not in him"* (Vs. 15).
- **Lust and pride are evil** – *"For all that is in the world--the lust of the flesh, the lust of the eyes, and the pride of life--is not of the Father but is of the world"* (Vs. 16).
- **Learn to do the will of God** – *"The world is passing away, and the lust of it; but he who does the will of God abides forever"* (Vs. 17).

"If there's ever been a time to rise up Church, it's now. As the blood bought saints of the living God proclaim, it's time to sound the alarm from the Church house to the White House and say, "We want God in America again." I believe it's time for America to stand up and proclaim, that one nation under God is our demand and send this evil lifestyle back to Satan where it came from and let the Word of God revive our dying land. Jesus Christ is coming back again in all His glory, and every eye shall see Him on that day.

That's why a new anointing of God's power's coming on us to boldly tell the world you must be saved. Because astrology won't save you, your horoscope won't save you; the Bible says these things are all a farce. If you're born again, you don't need to look to the stars for your answers, 'cause you can look to the very One who made those stars. History tells us time and time again, to live like there's no God makes you a fool. If you want to see kids live right stop handing out condoms and start handing out the Word of God in schools" (America Again by Carman).

Surrendering our hearts to the Lord is the only way to save our nation. Biblical morality is the key to saving our children, our marriages, and our churches. Immorality is a destroyer of everything good. It is the culprit behind the destruction of a person's heart. Living in the shadows of this lane will ruin everything. God's Word makes it clear. *"Put on the Lord Jesus Christ, and make no provision for the flesh, to fulfill its lusts"* (Rom. 13:14). It's time to come out of the gray and back to light, because Jesus said, *"I am the light of the world. He who follows Me shall not walk in darkness, but have the light of life"* (John 8:12).

I want to end this section with the chorus of Carman's song, *America Again*, "The only hope for America is Jesus. The only hope for our country is Him. If we repent of our ways, stand firm and say we need God in America again."

It's time to make a change and get off this road and lane.
See "God's plan for you" at the back of this book.

> *"To get a nation back on their feet, we must first get down on our knees" –Billy Graham*

The Sorcerers

Malachi 3:5 (NKJV)
"And I will come near you for judgment; I will be a swift witness Against sorcerers, Against adulterers, Against perjurers...Because they do not fear Me," Says the LORD of hosts."

LANE
6

Lane Six – The SORCERERS AND MAGIC ARTS

In the Old Testament God deals severely with those who engage in sorcery and magic arts. In Exodus 22:18 God's Law was clear and precise, *"You shall not permit a sorceress to live."* In Leviticus 19:31 (NIV) the inquirers of such evil would suffer too. *"Do not turn to mediums or seek out spiritists, for you will be defiled by them. I am the LORD your God."* A great reason Christians are falling away from the Lord in record numbers has much to do with our curiosity with psychics and mediums. Livescience.com reports some scary stats: (1) 71% of people say they have had a paranormal experience. (2) 56% believe that ghosts are spirits of the dead. (3) 21% believe in witches. People who have tapped into these demonic arenas are in danger spiritually. Titus 1:15-16 says, *"To the pure all things are pure, but to those who are defiled and unbelieving nothing is pure; but even their mind and conscience are defiled. They profess to know God, but in works they deny Him, being abominable, disobedient, and disqualified for every good work."* A defiled man is in a difficult place with God. In Charles H. Spurgeon's sermon called, *Defiled and Defiling* he said, "Every man whose heart is not renewed by Grace is in this sad and terrible condition!"

What about nations? A good argument for the spiritual decline in America is our overall infatuation to seek advice and direction from psychics and mediums. The entertainment industry continually bombards us with television shows glamourizing unexplained phenomenon such as: mysterious disappearances, intuition, creatures and monsters, ghosts, déjà vu, UFOs, near death experiences, life after death experiences, psychic powers, ESP, and others. These things and others keep the focus off God and the Bible. One day, as I was sitting in a local restaurant two women were discussing aliens. I was shocked to learn that sometime this year, although she wasn't for sure if it would be this year, an alien race would land on earth. These aliens, who have been around for a long time, have been watching us. She described that only those who are enlightened can see their

ships; which are like the stars in the sky. With confidence she explained that they are here to help us. When they come they are planning to transform us in all ways; even our broken down bodies to perfect health.

Anytime the Creator is taken out of the equation it's never good for that nation. America has all but thrown Jesus and the Word of God under the bus. When people become defiled, it is a matter of time for the nation to experience the same. America has reached a tipping point. Long ago, God sent His word to the prophet Haggai. His warning to the defiled and unclean is for us today. *"If one who is unclean because of a dead body touches any of these, will it be unclean?"* So the priests answered and said, *"It shall be unclean."* Then Haggai answered and said, *" 'So is this people, and so is this nation before Me,' says the Lord, 'and so is every work of their hands; and what they offer there is unclean."* We too have touched what the Lord considers unclean; psychics, mediums, sorcerers, and magic arts.

Once upon a time, there was an outbreak of witches and witchcraft. A formal persecution erupted in the early American colonies and in Europe at large from around 1450 to 1750. It included the sporadic killing of women on the account of suspected practice of witchcraft. Today, witchcraft has morphed into many different practices. In America we have become desensitized to it, but witchcraft still scares some. In 1928 a family of Hungarian peasants was acquitted of beating an old woman to death whom they claimed was a witch. In her book, *The Dark Side of Christian History*, Helen Ellerbe shares the following story, "In 1976 a poor woman, Elizabeth Hahn, was suspected of witchcraft and of keeping familiars, or devil's agents, in the form of dogs. In her small German village, the people ostracized her, threw rocks at her, and threatened to beat her to death before burning her house, badly burning her and killing her animals."

> *America has all but thrown Jesus and the Word of God under the bus*

Clearly, witch hunts are a thing of the past. It appears God isn't asking anyone to take out David Copperfield, Chris Angel or David Blaine; who generally do acts of illusion. So, what does the Father expect from His children today? According to the Bible of Dictionary Themes, "The attempt to discover or influence the future by means forbidden by God, including the use of divination, astrology or witchcraft. Such practices are strongly condemned in Scripture." The question is what do we do about it? Basically, the only time we use or hear the words, *witches and sorcerers* are in movies and television. While they exist, real-life witches, and devil worshipers must be hiding in plain sight. When I was in Bible College, one of my professors said, "Every Tuesday night the Satanic church prays against pastors and their families." While the evil doers on this lane are not easy to see, this lane remains a central thoroughfare, saturating our culture and society.

While most want to know what the future holds, the danger is trusting in some false belief to reveal it. Looking to astrology, witchcraft, devil worship, spiritism, séances, palm reading, fortune telling, and all other forms of this kind of evil, are not on God's approved list. These evil practices claim to reveal the future and control a person's fate, life, and destiny. Sadly, in their search for answers, unbelievers don't see the Bible as relevant. What about believers? People of biblical faith may not live on this lane, but some like to dabble. Experimenting with these forms of magic is dangerous. Yielding control to anything other than Christ is very hazardous.

These things are considered *"Works of the flesh"* (Gal. 5:20). Just before this verse, in Galatians 5:16-17 Paul warns us, *"So I say, walk by the Spirit, and you will not gratify the desires of the flesh. For the flesh desires what is contrary to the Spirit, and the Spirit what is contrary to the flesh. They are in conflict with each other, so that you are not to do whatever you want."* It's important to understand the effect these evil practices can have on the believer. Especially for weak-minded believers, these *"Works of the flesh"* can lead to falling away from the faith.

Sorcery, the use of spells, divination, or speaking to spirits, is clearly condemned in the Bible. The word sorcery in Scripture is always used in reference to an evil or deceptive practice. Here are a few Bible verses to consider:

- **Witchcraft is a work of the flesh** – *"Now the works of the flesh are manifest, which are these; Adultery, fornication, uncleanness, lasciviousness, idolatry, witchcraft"* (Gal. 5:20).

- **Satan will used false signs and wonders in the end-times** – *"The coming of the lawless one is by the activity of Satan with all power and false signs and wonders"* (2 Thess. 2:9 ESV).
- **Consulting them make God angry** – *"Consulted mediums and spiritists. He did much evil in the eyes of the Lord, arousing his anger"* (2 Chron. 33:36 NIV).
- **We should inquire of God** – *"When someone tells you to consult mediums and spiritists, who whisper and mutter, should not a people inquire of their God? Why consult the dead on behalf of the living?"* (Isaiah 8:19 NIV).
- **These things are in vain** – *"Fortune-tellers predict only lies, and interpreters of dreams pronounce falsehoods that give no comfort. So my people are wandering like lost sheep; they are attacked because they have no shepherd"* (Zec. 10:2 NLT).

In Acts 8:9, the King James Bible says, *"A certain man, called Simon, which before time in the same city used sorcery, and bewitched the people of Samaria."* This man was able to amaze the people of Samaria. As well, American's are enamored by people like Simon? In America, lane 6 has become a powerful industry shaping the culture. Magic is everywhere. Our children see it through Disney cartoons; which promote fairies, magic spells, sorcerers, witches and all kinds of mystical creatures. It's all around us; everywhere you look from movies like, Disney's *Mickey Mouse and the Sorcerer's Apprentice*, to *Harry Potter and the Hogwarts School of Witchcraft and Wizardry*. Magic is beamed into our lives via television sitcoms like *I Dream of Jeanie*, *Bewitched*, and *Wizards of Waverly Place*. In newspapers, and on the internet, anyone needing direction for the day can read their daily horoscope. For some that does the trick. In most cities, you can find a local palm reader or fortune teller by driving through the city. Even the highest office in our land, the Presidency, has succumbed to the use of witchcraft and divination. The Bible divides this lane into four areas: practicing magic, divination, spiritism and astrology.

Practicing Magic

Wicca is a religion based on early West European paganism. While Wiccan beliefs vary, depending on the individual, the focus isn't on the God of the Bible. Wiccan's look to other systems and gods to encourage self-discipline, self-awareness, rituals, personal power, responsibility, and freedom of choice. "Witchcraft, in the modern sense of the word, is a catch-all term to describe the practice of magic, especially magic that focuses on self, the Earth, and animistic spirits, rather than demons, angels, and other such extra planar entities" (wikiHow.com).

Divination

From ancient times, people looked to divination to gain understanding of future events. It is a Latin word meaning *divinare*, "to foresee" or "to be inspired by a god." Biblically, *"The sin of divination"* (1 Sam. 15:10) is rebellion. As Christians our wisdom should come from God (James 1:5), not by other supernatural means. God the Creator deserves our heart and allegiance. Divination was one of the reasons Israel was exiled in the first place (2 Kings 17:17). Divination has many forms in our modern culture. Some include consulting the horoscope, the casting of symbols, reading tarot cards, playing with Ouija board games, interpreting tea leaves, etc.

Spiritism

One man said, "Spiritism is a religion for the spiritual, but not the religious." We know that the spirit world is made up of both angelic and demonic forces (Eph. 6). These forces are in a war for the souls of man. The Bible says, *"Believe not every spirit, but try the spirits"* (1 John 4:1). We test spirits to see if they are of God. Followers of Spiritism used mediums, psychics and guides to communicate with the dead. They seek spirit-revelations to find greater happiness in life, plus a good incarnation for the next life. In Deuteronomy 18:9-11, this is considered an evil practice. *"There shall not be found among you anyone who makes his son or his daughter pass through the fire, or one who practices witchcraft, or a soothsayer, or one who interprets omens, or a sorcerer, or one who conjures spells, or a medium, or a spiritist, or one who calls up the dead."*

Astrology

It's most commonly used as a means of divination, by which future events are predicted. The Encyclopedia of the Bible explains astrology as, "The observation of sun, moon, planets, and stars for the purpose of determining the character of individuals and the course of events. The data used by astrology are the movements of the heavenly bodies, specifically, those which appear in the circle of twelve constellations, the zodiac. The sun regularly cuts a path, called the ecliptic, across the zodiac. The planets move in and out of this sector at various intervals." In contrast, students of scripture know, *"By Him all things were created that are in heaven and that are on earth, visible and invisible, whether thrones or dominions or principalities or powers. All things were created through Him and for Him. And He is before all things, and in*

Him all things consist" (Col. 1:16-17). Long before Thales, Aristotle, Ptolemy, al-Khwarizmi, Copernicus, Galileo, Newton, Einstein, Hubble, Hoyle, Hawking, and many others, Almighty God placed the stars into place (Gen. 1:17), and counted the number of stars; and *"Calls them all by name"* (Psalm 147:4). People have always been fascinated with the universe; the stars, galaxies, patterns and movements. As tiny pieces of the overall puzzle, mankind strives to find his purpose and meaning. Our purpose must be found in relationship with Christ because, *"In Him we live and move and have our being"* (Acts 17:28). Jeremiah warned the people *"Do not be dismayed at the signs of the heavens"* (Jer. 10:2). The root of this evil practice is because people of all cultures, ancient and modern, *"look skyward to find the face of the divine"* (Molly Hall).

Sorcery and the Drug Culture

There is one more interesting thing about the word sorcery. The New Testament Greek word translated "sorcery" is *pharmakeia*. Our English word "pharmacy" is derived from it. "In Paul's day, the word primarily meant 'dealing in poison' or 'drug use' and was applied to divination and spell-casting because sorcerers often used drugs along with their incantations and amulets to conjure occult power" (gotquestions.org).

Drug use is on the rise in our land. The lines between legal and illegal are continuing to be blurred today. America continues to push and provoke God with this evil offshoot of sorcery. The human body was created to be the *"Temple of the Holy Spirit"* (1 Cor. 6:19). In fact, *"God created man in His own image; in the image of God He created him; male and female He created them"* (Gen. 1:26). This lane has led to the abuse of the human body; physically, mentally and spiritually. Drugs and other substances have begun to conquer the minds of Americans. In the garden *"God blessed them, and God said to them, 'Be fruitful and multiply; fill the earth and subdue it; have dominion over the fish of the sea, over the birds of the air, and over every living thing that moves on the earth.'"* (Gen. 1:27). The exact opposite view is blossoming. When fish, birds, other living things take precedence over mankind, we are living in disobedience. When drugs, for recreational use are applauded and celebrated, God is not pleased. The minds of Americans are being weakened and destroyed by marijuana and other gateway drugs. Those who pick up a joint instead of the Word of God are receiving a temporary high, instead of the ultimate high, a relationship with Jesus.

Lane six is for those who have received the *"Spirit of the world"* (1 Cor. 1:12), rather than the *"Spirit who is from God, that we might know the things that have been freely given to us by God"* (1 Cor. 1:12). America is blind to the fact that the earth has dominion over us. The war on drugs is a world war surly, but America seems to be losing the battle for the minds of its citizens. The National Institute on Drug Abuse (NIDA) says, "Drugs change the brain in ways that foster compulsive drug abuse, quitting is difficult, even for those who are ready to do so." The battle is for the mind. 1 Corinthians 1:15-16 says, *"But the natural man does not receive the things of the Spirit of God, for they are foolishness to him; nor can he know them, because they are spiritually discerned. But he who is spiritual judges all things, yet he himself is rightly judged by no* one. For 'who has known the mind of the Lord that he may instruct Him?' But we have the mind of Christ."

According to *USA Today*, "Twenty states

America is losing the war for the minds of her citizens

plus the District of Columbia have enacted laws that allow people to use medical marijuana with a doctor's recommendation." Any honest person understands that medical marijuana is a stepping stone for the proponents of legalizing the substance. Confirmation came in 2013 when both Washington and Colorado voted to legalize the use of recreational Marijuana. This speckle will only escalate. In their attempt to generate more revenue, Washington and Colorado has further alienated themselves from God's protection and blessings. There decisions are a direct slap in the face to God and His Word. Already, the problem is escalating. In Colorado, a fourth grader sold edible pot to three other children for eleven dollars. The child apparently stole the pot from his grandparents.

Soon the need for the next high or the next new drug will raise its ugly head. The fun will be over and the real problems will take center stage. As one thing leads to another, the next drug will be exponentially worse. When the evil at work has its way, all drugs will be openly sold on the streets. Finally, all drugs will be legal and America will wish she had the moral conviction to stop it when she could of.

According to the National Council of Alcoholism and Drug Dependence, "80% of inmates abuse drugs or alcohol. 50% of inmates are clinically addicted. 60% of inmates tested positive for illegal drugs at time of their arrest, and about 21% of inmates are incarcerated for non-violent drug crimes.

Even Christians struggle with the use and abuse of drugs and alcohol. Why are believers inundated with substance abuse? Unfortunately, the gradual alterations of the mind over time have kept many from becoming a serious part of the Body of Christ. Drugs and alcohol have their claws inside the local church. Despite the obvious side effects and what the written Word of God says, many believers struggle with substances. An incredible article in *Black Media Scoop* might shock you. It is reported that "A pastor in Kentucky is accused of running the largest pill trafficking organization in the state. Neighbors are shocked to find out that the preacher wasn't as much into praising God as he was into selling dope." This is further proof the Body of Christ is falling away from the faith. The article goes on to say, "Police say that the pastor hid the drugs inside the wall of a room that looked like a playroom for children. Tens of thousands of pills that have a street value of $40 to $45 each." If a pastor would engage in something so evil, think about what others might do?

The dangers of this lane aren't only for the obvious Satanists, Wiccans, Fortune Tellers, etc, but for the people sitting in the pews every Sunday. We must raise our spiritual antennas and pay closer attention. In the article *Types of Magic* by Catherine Beyer she says, "Defining types of magic is just as complicated as defining magic itself. In common usage, magic evokes some sort of change in the physical world through non-scientific means. In occult and esoteric circles, 'magic' can take a wider meaning involving spiritual change."

The God shaped hole in all of us can only be filled with God's love through Jesus Christ. Seeking answers apart from God and His Word ruin us over time. Opening the mind to evil spirits, ultimately closes our mind to the things of God. Being in Christ

Danny L. Formhals Sr.

means to *"Set your mind on things above, not on things on the earth. For you died, and your life is hidden with Christ in God"* (Col. 3:2-3). Those who try to fill the void in their lives with sorcery, magic, and substances, create a huge spiritual problem for themselves. Watchman Nee said, "Feelings change as the world changes. Their easy excitement can occasion a saint to lose his spiritual balance. Their constant disturbance can affect a believer's peace in his spirit."

It's time to make a change and get off this road and lane.
See "God's plan for you" at the back of this book.

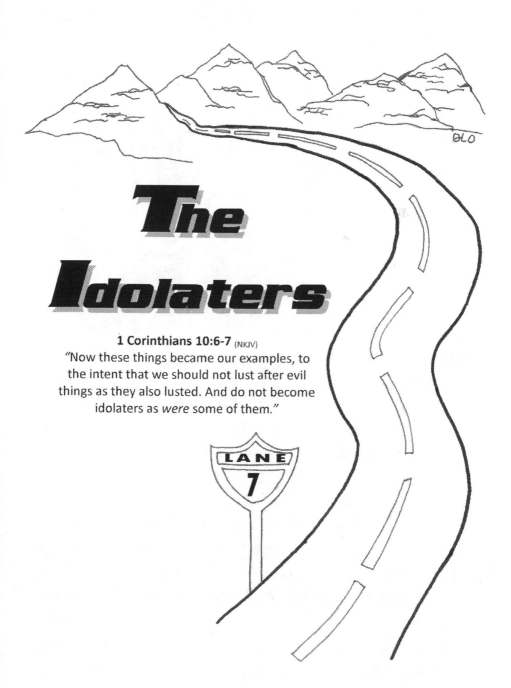

The Idolaters

1 Corinthians 10:6-7 (NKJV)
"Now these things became our examples, to the intent that we should not lust after evil things as they also lusted. And do not become idolaters as *were* some of them."

LANE

7

Lane Seven – The IDOLATERS

This lane, like the others leads to a Godless eternity. Idolatry is defined as, "The worship of a physical object as a god" (M-W.com). These travelers walk about like nomads, they have no specific home. They worship the creation instead of the Creator. They have completely missed it; God and His purpose for them. I compare them to the person whose ship finally came in, but they were at the airport instead

of the dock. This godless group has greatly disappointed God.

The first two Commandments are greater proof idolatry is a deal breaker to the Father. First, *"You shall have no other gods before Me"* (Ex. 20:3). Second, *"You shall not make for yourself a carved image--any likeness of anything that is in heaven above, or that is in the earth beneath, or that is in the water under the earth; you shall not bow down to them nor serve them"* (Ex. 20:4-5). Some want to disregard the Old Testament, or put it in the back seat. Do the first two Laws of Moses apply to our lives today? I answer that question by looking at what Jesus and the New Testament writers said about the law. One of the mistakes we make as students of scripture is failing to allow the Word of God to interpret itself. In other words, the Bible is: inspired (2 Tim. 3:16), infallible (Acts 1:3), perfect (Prov. 30:5), and inerrant (Rom. 3:4). Applying the wisdom of man makes it easy to assume meanings which have been handed down to us. This makes it possible to miss what Jesus and the nearly 40 other writers of the Bible have said. Simply put, the Bible does not contradict itself, despite what critics would want you to believe. With the help of an article in RGC.org titled, *Does the New Testament Teach All Ten Commandments?* I put together a list of New Testament references back to the Mosaic Law. As you read them, study them and keep an open mind, you will see what Jesus meant when He said, *"Do not think that I came to destroy the Law or the Prophets. I did not come to destroy but to fulfill"* (Matthew 5:17). Clearly, the New Testament writers addressed all Ten of the Commandments.

The Mosaic Law in the New Testament

- **Matthew 7:12** – The golden rule, "do unto others" confirms the Law and Prophets.
- **Matthew 15:18-19** – Jesus speaks of defilement referring to the Sixth, Ninth, and Third Commandments.
- **Matthew 19:18-19** – Jesus speaks to *"Keeping the commandments"* referring to the Sixth, Seventh, Eighth, Ninth, and Fifth Commandments.
- **Matthew 22:36-40** – Jesus speaks to the Greatest Commandment, which all the law and prophets hinge on.
- **Mark 7:1-13** – Jesus charged the religious leaders of the times with abandoning the Law for the tradition of men.
- **Luke 4:8** – When tempted by the Devil, Jesus referred to the First Commandment.
- **Luke 4:16** – A reference to the Fourth Commandment to *"Keep the Sabbath holy"* (Luke 6:5; Acts 17:2; 13:42-43; Heb. 4:9).
- **Romans 7:7** – Paul refers to the Tenth Commandment and coveting.

- **Romans 13:8-9** – Paul lists several Commandments in regards to loving your neighbor.
- **Romans 13:10** – Love fulfills the law.
- **1 Corinthians 11:1** – The Apostle Paul states, *"Follow me as I follow Christ."*
- **Ephesians 2:9-10** – God created us for good works, which require rules to follow.
- **Ephesians 4:25** – Paul refers to lying, which is a reference to the Ninth Commandment.
- **Ephesians 6:2** – The Apostle Paul refers to honoring parents, the Fifth Commandment.
- **Colossians 3:8** – Paul refers to the Third Commandment of blasphemy (see Lev. 24:16).
- **1 Peter 2:21** – We are called to follow in Christ's steps, who didn't break the law and sin.
- **James 1:14-15** – James refers to the dangers of coveting, the Tenth Commandment.
- **1 John 2:3-6** – The proof we know Christ is by keeping His word and commandments.
- **1 John 5:2-3** – We love God if we keep His commandments, which reinforces them all.
- **2 John 5-6** – To love God means to obey all His commandments. This is not a new Command.

The 10 Commandments

1. Other god's	6. Murder
2. Idol worship	7. Adultery
3. God's name in vain	8. Stealing
4. Sabbath day holy	9. False witness
5. Honor parents	10. Coveting

Idolatry – Breaking the Second Commandment

- **The Second Commandment** – Exodus 20:4-6 *"You shall not make for yourself a carved image, or any likeness of anything that is in heaven above, or that is in the earth beneath, or that is in the water under the earth; you shall not bow down to them nor serve them. For I, the Lord your God, am a jealous God, visiting the iniquity of the fathers on the children to the third and fourth generations of those who hate Me, but showing mercy to thousands, to those who love Me and keep My commandments."*

- **Jesus instructing us how to worship God** – John 4:24 *"God is Spirit, and those who worship Him must worship in spirit and truth."*

- **The Apostle Paul warning about worshiping idols** – 1 Corinthians 10:7 *"And do not become idolaters as were some of them. As it is written, "The people sat down to eat and drink, and rose up to play."*

- **Idol worship is to deny the truth of God** – Romans 1:25 *"who exchanged the truth of God for the lie, and worshiped and served the creature rather than the Creator, who is blessed forever. Amen."*

- **Idol worshippers have no part in the Kingdom of God** – Ephesians 5:5 *"For this you know, that no fornicator, unclean person, nor covetous man, who is an idolater, has any inheritance in the kingdom of Christ and God."*
- **Idol worship is a lifestyle** – Galatians 5:19-21 *"When you follow the desires of your sinful nature, the results are very clear: sexual immorality, impurity, lustful pleasures, idolatry, sorcery, hostility, quarreling, jealousy, outbursts of anger, selfish ambition, dissension, division, envy, drunkenness, wild parties, and other sins like these. Let me tell you again, as I have before, that anyone living that sort of life will not inherit the Kingdom of God.*

The idolaters daily break the Second Commandment. All those without Christ thrive here, but what about those who call themselves Christians? What things do we put before the Lord? There have been seasons in my life, maybe yours also, where I have put something before God. A person or a thing in front of God is idolatry. Look around you; its obvious things and lifestyle are more important than God. Young people worship celebrities, a video game or playing a sport. Adults worship money, people, or a job. Our relationship with God suffers when these things come before God. Growing up, there were countless times I declared, "I love the Lord with all my heart." This was a lie because I was deceived and allowed people and things to become idols. Idols can be made with one's hands or just conceived in one's mind. To have an image of what God is like and worship or follow that image is evil in the Lord's eyes. According to *The Practical Word Studies in the New Testament*, the word idolatry means, "Both the worship of false gods and the failure to have a right relationship with God. Any person who does not worship God is worshipping some idol, and almost everything upon earth can become an idol and consume the heart and passion of man." It's a dangerous thing to give our primary attention and devotion to someone or something other than God.

The history of the Children of Israel and the modern Christian proves that we struggle with God's standard; which is giving our all to God first. When Jesus said, *"You shall love the Lord your God with all your heart, with all your soul, and with all your mind"* (Matt. 22:37), He was actually referring back to the time when the children of Israel were about to enter the Promise Land. God said, *"Hear, O Israel: The Lord our God, the Lord is one! You shall love the Lord your God with all your heart, with all your soul, and with all your strength. And these words which I command you today shall be in your heart. You shall teach them diligently to your children, and shall talk of them when you sit in your house, when you walk by the way, when you lie down, and when you rise up. You shall bind them as a sign on your hand, and they shall be as frontlets between your eyes. You shall write them on the doorposts of your house and on your gates"* (Duet. 6:4-9). The high standard of *all* should be in our hearts.

The nation of India is known as the land of 330 million gods. Considering, as of 2014 the population of the United States was 317 million people, each person could worship their own god, with room to spare. 330 million gods is a lot, even for India's 1.27 billion people. The first time I travelled to India, I saw firsthand several gods being worshiped. Statues, temples and acts of worship were everywhere; even on the streets. It was truly amazing being there and witnessing that.

Danny L. Formhals Sr.

As our team travelled four hours to a little village, I asked the host pastor about why there were so many gods. As a believer in Jesus Christ, he once himself worshiped several gods. He didn't know the history of some of the gods he worshipped, but bowed to them anyway. He stated that most Indians don't know what they are worshiping, nor why? Traditions have been pasted down, so the people worship in ignorance. To prove his point he related the following story about one of the gods people worship. He couldn't recall the name, but I named it *The Dung god of India.* It goes like this: "One day a woman was walking her child along the road. The child had to use the bathroom, so the mother took her child about 10 feet off the road. After the child finished doing its business the mother had a thought. She said to herself, 'This was a special moment and it should be remembered.' So, she quickly found some flowers and went back and placed them on the very spot. Then she went on her way. Later that day someone happened to see the flowers and thought, 'Something special happened here.' So, that person placed additional flowers on the spot. Later another came, and seeing all the flowers, decided to contribute to the occasion and erected a little stone shelter over the spot. Still another came and made a larger stone monument. Finally, a wealthy person heard about the little memorial and made a large shrine; where people could come say a prayer. Today, the people go to a place to worship, pray and ask a god they don't know, to bless them. They have no clue how the shrine and *Dung god* was started." Sadly, people all over the world worship foolish so-called gods who can only give them warm fuzziest, but not really help them.

The early church dealt with Idolatry. According to the Life Application Bible Notes, "Idol worship was the major expression of religion in Corinth." Paul warns the church to run away from it (1 Cor. 10:14). To the church in Ephesus he warns them to not take God's kingdom lightly (Eph. 5:5). To the Galatians, Paul expresses that idol worship is a lifestyle (Gal. 5:21). A closer look at Ephesians 5:5 reveals an interesting comment about the Kingdom of God. *"For this you know, that no fornicator, unclean person, nor covetous man, who is an idolater, has any inheritance in the kingdom of Christ and God."* What a horrible thing to be excluded from the kingdom of Christ and God. I find it fascinating how Paul emphasizes *"Christ and God"* in the passage. These are not two distinct kingdoms, for the Bible has several names for the Kingdom of God. I want to draw a comparison to the idol worship as a lifestyle and as an occasional thing. In other words, how is idolatry different for the sinner and the saint? One thing for sure, walking in this lane will change our standing in God's kingdom.

In **THE KINGDOM OF CHRIST**, entrance begins with a relationship with Jesus. Speaking to the Pharisees Jesus said, *"The kingdom of God is within you"* (Luke 17:21). We are called to *"Be followers of God"* (Eph. 5:1). To live a powerful and effective Christian life, we must *"Seek first the kingdom of God and His righteousness, and all these things shall be added to you"* (Matt. 6:33). Idolatry will hinder and eventually ruin a person's walk with Christ.

In **THE KINGDOM OF GOD** there are three groups of idolaters who will miss out on eternal life. These people choose to worship other things rather than God.

- **Some will never come into His Kingdom** – The Bible is clear, Jesus came to *"Seek and to save the lost"* (Luke 19:10). Sadly, many will disregard His efforts. Even though Jesus came to die for their sins (Rom. 4:25), they refuse to worship Him. Tragically, these people will die in their sins (John 8:24), which means they die spiritually, which is the second death (Rev. 20:14).

- **Some reason they are in His Kingdom, but are not** – There are those who know God in their head, thinking are going to heaven. In reality, they don't know God at all (Matt. 7:21-23). We must know Him intimately, not just know about Him. This is going from the knowledge of God to a relationship with God, through Jesus His Son. This transformation takes the believer from religion to relationship.

- **Some will leave His Kingdom** – There are those who came into the kingdom and left it. Some would argue that these people were never believers in the first place. This is a feeble argument because the Word of God is populated with far too many examples and verses about falling away, losing the faith and more. According to the parable of the sower, lasting salvation depends on where the seed falls. In Matthew 13, according to the parable of the sower, it is possible for the Word to take hold until the cares of life choke it out. What the new believer does with the seed, *"The gift of eternal life"* (Rom. 6:23) is what makes the difference. Entrance into God's eternity is certain for believers who have their names written in the Book of Life (Rev. 20:15). Idolatry robs the believer of all of God's free gifts. Idolatry is a tool the devil uses to weaken and destroy the believer's faith. Dan Corner said it like this, "God is faithful to us (1 John 1:9; 1 Cor. 10:13) but we must be faithful to him to the very end of our lives to escape the lake of fire or second death (Rev. 2:10-11)." Let me say it, yes, I believe we must *"Keep the faith"* (2 Cor. 5:7) and *"Die daily"* (1 Cor. 15:51) or we are endanger of walking away from God. God will never leave us (Heb. 13:5), but we can leave Him (Rev. 2:4). God assuredly loves us (Rom. 8:35-39) but those who inherit the kingdom of God must love God (James 2:5) and to love God means to obey his commands (John 14:15; 1 John 5:3). When someone worships idols, they fail to obey God and prove they don't really love Him. Will they inherit the kingdom of God? It's time believers do the math and consider the cost (Luke 14:28).

Those who fail to repent of the sin of idolatry are losing their relationship with Jesus Christ, and potentially will be left out of heaven. King Solomon struggled with idolatry, we must become more aware. In 1 Kings 11:11 the Lord said to Solomon *"Because you have done this, and have not kept My covenant and My statutes, which I have commanded you, I will surely tear the kingdom away from you and give it to your servant."* Don't be shocked, If the smartest man to have ever lived could lose a kingdom, so could we. Not only did Solomon blow it, but the people of Jeremiah's time as well. They decided to build sacrificial fires, make food and pour out liquid offering to idol gods. Let this nation and people be warned and hear what the Lord says, *"Am I the one they are hurting?"* asks the Lord. *"Most of all, they hurt themselves, to their own shame."* So this is what the Sovereign Lord says: *"I will pour out my terrible fury on this place. Its people,*

> *If the smartest man to have ever lived could lose a kingdom, so could we*

animals, trees, and crops will be consumed by the unquenchable fire of my anger" (Jer. 7:18-20).

It's time to make a change and get off this road and lane.
See "God's plan for you" at the back of this book.

The Liars

1 Peter 3:10 (NKJV)
"For "He who would love life And see good days, Let him refrain his tongue from evil, And his lips from speaking deceit."

LANE
8

Lane Eight – The LIARS

This is a very popular lane on the abysmal 8-lane highway; possibly the most travelled. 100% of us have lied and continue to bend the truth on a regular basis. If lies could take form and be seen the skies would be littered with them. The sun wouldn't shine through for all the lies floating around. A liar comes in all shapes and sizes; from rookies to pros.

Children don't have to be taught to lie, it comes natural. Regardless of the chocolate evidence all over the child's face, denying the existence of the missing candy bar becomes as natural as taking a breath. According to *WorldNetDaily,* "A new

survey shows the average person tells 4 lies a day, or 1,460 a year for a total of 88,000 by the age of 60." The same article goes go to show that the most common lie is, "I'm fine." Lies are a normal part of life, both for believers and unbelievers. Certainly, we should seek a different path. Lying is like slapping Jesus and the Bible across the face. After all, Jesus is *"The Truth"* (John 14:6), and the *"Word is truth"* (John 17:17). Sadly, for some lying has become as natural as breathing. Their lifestyle of constant lying has put them in great danger. The danger is that they come to a point where they start to believe their own lies.

The Eighth Commandment given to Moses says, *"You shall not bear false witness against your neighbor"* (Ex. 20:16). Lying is such an offense to God; that He would put it in His original top ten. This form of lying hurts and can destroy others. Do all lies damage others? I admit there are some lies that, on the surface, seem beneficial. One internet website says, "The beneficial lie is used by a person who intends to help others. For example, a farmer hiding Jews from Nazis who is asked if he's keeping any Jews in his house is seen as acting heroically when he lies. The rescue worker who pulls a child from the remains of a burning car and lies to the child that his mother and father are OK is saving the child, in the short term, from more traumas. Doctors who lie to a patient on their deathbed to lift their spirits or prescribe fake meditation, placebos, to patients are also technically lying" (TheUnboundSpirit.com).

Maybe these are not really counted as lies; when genuine protection is paramount. Regardless, lying in most cases is to gain a selfish edge. Assuredly, lying comes in many forms. This list was adapted from Dawson McAllister's, *The Different Kinds of Lies You Tell*, and Eva Rykrsmith's article, *Know when someone is lying*. Take a pencil and put a check mark by those you have participated in your lifetime.

- **White lie:** Called the least serious of lies. People tell them claiming to be tactful or polite.
- **Broken promise:** A failure to keep one's spoken commitment or promise.
- **Gossip/Fabrication:** Telling something you don't know for sure is true.

- **Bold-faced lie:** Telling something that everyone knows is a lie.
- **Exaggeration:** Enhancing a truth by adding lies to it, to make something appear better.
- **Deception:** Creating an impression that causes others to be misled, not telling all the facts.
- **Plagiarism:** Copying someone else's work and calling it your own.
- **Compulsive lying:** A failure to stop lying even when the truth is easier and better.
- **Error:** Lying by mistake or ignorance.
- **Omission:** Leaving out relevant information, which is passive deception.
- **Restructuring:** Distorting context, using sarcasm, changing characters, or altering the scene.
- **Denial:** Refusing to acknowledge a truth.
- **Minimization:** Reduced the effects of a mistake, a fault, or a judgment call.

Wicked and malicious liars are determined to destroy their victims. The end game is the loss of character and reputation. Others lie to protect themselves and don't realize the ultimate consequences of their words. Like the boy who cried wolf, one lie can set the course of a young person's life forever. Abraham Lincoln once said, "You can fool some of the people all of the time, and all of the people some of the time, but you cannot fool all of the people all of the time." When Satan spewed his half-truths, in the Garden of Eden, sin began to corrupt a perfect world. When Adam and Eve embraced the lies and were deceived everything changed.

The French conqueror Napoleon said, "History is a set of lies agreed upon." The time has come to recognize the lies from the truth. If we agree to lie or follow after lies, we are susceptible to the same corruption the first couple experienced. We will potentially not only lose paradise, but the many blessings of God's creation. Have we become like the scorpion who hitched a ride from the fox to cross the river. He promised not to sting the fox, but halfway out, the scorpion did what it does best. "Why did you sting me?" the fox declared. The scorpion said, "It is my nature to sting." When Satan lies, he is only doing what he does best. When individuals lie, they are replicating the father of lies. Jesus exposes Satan's character in a sermon he preached in John 8:44. He said, *"He was a murderer from the beginning, and does not stand in the truth, because there is no truth in him. When he speaks a lie, he speaks from his own resources, for he is a liar and the father of it."* Maybe you're simply the victim, the fox. Either way, lies rob, kill and destroy everything.

Liars become pawns in Satan's schemes. Do you know anybody who walked away from Christ, because someone in Christian circles lied to them? The greatest tragedy lies produce are those who walk away or never come to know Christ personally. Like the atomic bomb, the lie is one of Satan's most powerful weapons. It is a major theme all-throughout scripture. Even many of our Biblical heroes uses deception and lies to accomplish their objectives. Abraham lied to Pharaoh (Gen. 12:13) and to Abimelech (Gen. 20:2) to protect his own life. Peter told three lies; denying he knew Jesus (Matt. 26:69-75). Ananias and Sapphira lied to the Holy Spirit and dropped dead on the spot (Acts 5:1-11). Here are some other verses about lying.

- Satan is a liar (Genesis 3:4; John 8:44).
- Those who don't keep God commandments are liars (1 John 2:4).
- Those who hate others are liars (1 John 4:20).
- God cannot lie (Titus 1:2; Heb. 6:18).
- We should hate telling lies (Prov. 13:5).
- Pathological liars will go to hell (Rev. 21:8).
- God hates liars (Prov. 6:16-19).
- A poor man is better than a liar (Prov. 19:22).

It's stunning to read that *"God hates liars"* and *"Those who fail to keep God's laws are considered a liar."* Only when believers become consumed with the truth, can we rise above the destruction lying brings. Going against the *truth*, which is another name for Jesus Christ, is going against the God of the Bible. Liars, occasional or consistent are going against truth. Lying causes all kinds of problems and destroys what is precious to God, relationships. In John Gills Exposition of the Bible he says, "Those who speak lies in common talk; and that deliver out doctrinal lies, false doctrines, lies in hypocrisy; these are abominable unto God; as being contrary to his nature as the God of truth."

As a major offense to God, lying is evil. That is why lying has its own lane on the highway to hell. Remember the old game show, Truth or Consequences? People, especially Christians better tell the truth, or there will be consequences. Forgetting or ignoring that Jesus is the truth (John 14:6), and telling falsehoods is akin to being at war with the Savior. When His goals and plans for a lost world are disrupted, He takes it very seriously. When people lie to themselves, others, and to God He will step in. Anyone who aligns themselves with evil, will pay a heavy price. In

Psalm 63:11 "The mouth of them that speak lies shall be stopped." In Proverbs 19:5, "A false witness shall not be unpunished; and he that speaks lies shall not escape." Lying is a very serious charge in the Word of God. Telling occasional lies may not bring ruin, but those who live a lifestyle of lying will not be allowed to enter heaven. At the end of it all, when it is time for judgment, *"Nothing evil will be allowed to enter, nor anyone who practices shameful idolatry and dishonesty—but only those whose names are written in the Lamb's Book of Life"* (Rev. 21:27). Our prayer should be *"Deliver my soul, O LORD, from lying lips, and from a deceitful tongue"* (Ps. 120:2).

> "Liars and cheaters may score a few runs but they will never win the game" -Unknown

It's time to make a change and get off this road and lane.
See "God's plan for you" at the back of this book.

Chapter 7 – Wake-up Call

"Arise, get up, wake up, open your eyes, step out, move from where you are to where you need to be" –Jan Payne

No joking matter

I've learned that lost people matter to God. Our world is filled with them. The lost and hurting dominate society. People have been the walking wounded since the dawn of time. Even Jesus spent time with them. He was constantly getting into trouble with the religious folks because he would sometimes hang out with sinners. Not to condone their sin, but to help them and save them from their sin. Fixing people's lives was what Jesus was about and what He was good at. The hurting usually found a way to get to him. They would yell, try to touch Him and even climb trees to catch a glimpse. That's exactly what Zacchaeus did. *"When Jesus reached the spot, he looked up and said to him, 'Zacchaeus, come down immediately. I must stay at your house today.' All the people saw this and began to mutter, 'He has gone to be the guest of a "sinner* (Luke 19:5-7 _{NIV}). No matter who is hurting in this world, Jesus came to touch them. As His followers, we must understand that hurting people need Jesus, and we can help them find comfort underneath His *"Everlasting arms"* (Deut. 33:27).

A lot of lost and hurting people won't admit they need Jesus in their life. Down inside, in the heart, somehow they know something isn't right. They're in serious danger, but they believe everything is fine. They have become a house on fire. They don't see the flames or feel the heat, so they stay locked inside. Soon their house will be consumed and then it will be too late.

This is no joking matter. The lost and hurting need someone to yell, "Fire!" They need someone to say, "Jesus!"

Maybe you heard about the professor. Defiantly, he lectures day by day, "There is no God." Then one day, as he is teaching in his lecture room, he tried stepping down from the podium. Somehow he missed the first step and almost fell to the ground. As he stumbled he screamed, "O my God". At that moment, as the whole class of students burst out in laughter the reality of the human heart is finally revealed. Even the atheist knows there is a God. This man, like millions around the country and the world need an encounter with Jesus.

My book has two purposes; first to call people to repentance. People all around us are on the *8-lane Highway*. Secondly, this book is a strong warning to the Christian community, saying in the Spirit of love, "Wake up!" We cannot afford to sleep, we must redeem the time for *"The days are evil"* (Eph. 5:16). We must rise and shine (Isa. 60:1) for the glory of God is coming again soon.

Statistics says we spend about 10 minutes daily searching for something. Like the guy looking for his sun glasses; which are safe and secure on the top of his head. The decline in church attendance is proof people are asleep and not passionately searching for God. The lost and hurting don't naturally search for God. Most are trying other avenues to ease the stress, pain and loneliness they feel. What about those who don't consider themselves lost? Are they searching for God? Sadly, too many Christians have forgotten where to look; the Word of God and in the local church.

One particular Wednesday night just before church service began a young man came to ask for money. He came to the church searching for what he needed. Later the Holy Spirit spoke to my heart. That young man could have come inside and received exactly what he needed through Christ. That sums up our country right now. The lost and hurting seek what satisfies in the moment. Like the women at the well. She didn't understand that a relationship with Jesus is the *"Living Water"* (John 4:10-14) Jesus spoke of. We cannot afford to play games any longer; people are dying and going to hell. Jesus answered and said to her, *"Whoever drinks of this water will thirst again, but whoever drinks of the water that I shall give him will never thirst. But the water that I shall give him will become in him a fountain of water springing up into everlasting life."* The woman said to Him, *"Sir, give me this water, that I may not thirst, nor come here to draw."* The lost and hurting need a drink. Not what the drink the world offers, but a large, pure, tall, refreshing glass of Jesus.

What Jesus Wants

When did we (the Body of Christ) lose our passion and zeal to go church to get what we actually need; more of God? Clearly, what the people want is different than what Jesus wants. While the world calls for peace, Jesus calls for a sword. In Matthew 10:34 Jesus makes a perplexing statement. *"Do not think that I came to bring peace on earth. I did not come to bring peace but a sword. For I have come to 'set a man against his father, a daughter against her mother, and a daughter-in-law against her mother-in-law'; and 'a man's enemies will be those of his own household.'"* The sword Jesus is speaking of is the Word of God. The book of Hebrews tells us that a sword divides. *"For the word of God is living and powerful, and sharper than any two-edged sword, piercing even to the division of soul and spirit, and of joints and marrow, and is a discerner of the thoughts and intents of the heart"* (Heb. 4:12).

Jesus wants a strong line drawn in the sand. There must be a difference between His followers and everyone else. In fact, Jesus further states, *"He who loves father or mother more than Me is not worthy of Me. And he who loves son or daughter more than Me is not worthy of Me. And he who does not take his cross and follow after Me is not worthy of Me. He who finds his life will lose it, and he who loses his life for My sake will find it. He who receives you receives Me, and he who receives Me receives Him who sent Me"* (Matt. 10:36-40). Jesus wants His people to be unique. In many ways, we have become like the world. In 2 Corinthians 6:17 this thought is confirmed, *"Come out from among them and be separate, says the Lord. Do not touch what is unclean, and I will receive you."*

The Word of God hasn't changed

Have we missed it? When did Christians stop wanting the whole truth? When did preachers stop encompassing the whole gospel message in their sermons? When did the preachers stop turning every page of scripture? If we stop reading it, we stop preaching it. Some of our spiritual leaders are content to speak on Biblical love, grace, forgiveness, and how to be a better Christian. They do those topics with passion, but barely gloss over topics on sin, hell and judgment. The local church has changed, but the Word of God has not changed. People change, but *"Jesus Christ is the same yesterday, today, and forever"* (Heb. 13:8). There is a highway of difference between what preachers used to say and what comes out of their mouths today. One pastor in my area recently said, "Promoting God's love should be the only agenda Christians ever have." The only agenda! He means well, but His comments sell short the whole gospel.

More and more pastors and teachers tell the masses what they want to hear. The further people get away from God the less they want to be challenged about their failure to seek after God. Regardless of what the people want to hear, the duty of the pastor is to *"Preach the gospel"* (Mark 16:15). What people want isn't necessarily what God wants. People, Christian or not, resist being told how to live. Despite the transparency of scripture, they are not living by God's rules. Pastors and leaders who are short-sighted when it comes to delivering all of God's Word have forgotten a very simple principal. God doesn't change, nor has His message.

Yes, love is the overall message, but so is judgment. After all, the Word of God concludes with twelve chapters on judgment and boldly declares, *"For I testify to everyone who hears the words of the prophecy of this book: If anyone adds to these things, God will add to him the plagues that are written in this book; and if anyone takes away from the words of the book of this prophecy, God shall take away his part from the Book of Life, from the holy city, and from the things which are written in this book"* (Rev. 22:18-19).

When did the message change?

The messengers have changed, though not the message. One of my greatest disappointments with the current Christian culture is the dramatic shift away from scripture. It's like turning off a light switch. It doesn't matter how the Word is ignored or changed, when it happens there is darkness. One short season of darkness is enough to change everything in a person's life or church. Paul warned the backslidden church in Galatia about obeying the truth. Remember, that the gospel message, rooted in love, is the truth people desperately need to hear and know. Something has crept into the church, a false teaching, which isn't from God. Paul said, *"You ran well. Who hindered you from obeying the truth? This persuasion does not come from Him who calls you. A little leaven leavens the whole lump. I have confidence in you, in the Lord, that you will have no other mind; but he who troubles you shall bear his judgment, whoever he is"* (Gal. 5:7-10).

Imagine the millions including church leaders who will hear the words, "You ran well...but." These church leaders have allowed a little bit of leaven inside; which has distorted the whole. The Preacher's Outline and Sermon Bible Commentary says, "The Galatian churches had backslidden. They were turning away from the truth, from Jesus Christ Himself. In this passage, Paul makes one last appeal to them: obey the truth. The only hope for

> *"Many have become pros at stealing God's Word"* -DLF

the backslider is to turn back to Christ and obey the truth." In Paul's day, to turn from the truth, meant to disregard the teachings of Jesus and the disciples. Today, to turn from the truth, means to turn from scripture. This is happening at an alarming rate. Paul recognized the plight of many who would succumb to *"A different gospel."* In Galatians 1:6-7 he said, *"I marvel that you are turning away so soon from Him who called you in the grace of Christ, to a different gospel, which is not another; but there are some who trouble you and want to pervert the gospel of Christ."* The Bible and its message have been warped by those who promote a perverted gospel. One day, God will deal with those who have perverted or kept His Word from the people. It's like stealing God's Word.

> *"Is not My word like a fire?" Says the LORD, "And like a hammer that breaks the rock in pieces?* [30] *"Therefore behold, I am against the prophets," says the LORD, "who steal My words every one from his neighbor.* [31] *Behold, I am against the prophets," says the LORD, "who use their tongues and say, 'He says.'* - Jeremiah 23:29-31

What the Bible actually says matters. Colin Smith says, "The Bible begins in a garden, ends in a city and all the way through points us to Jesus." The Bible was written by over forty authors over about 1,500 years in three languages on three different continents yet has one central message coursing through it. So, what then is the overarching theme of the Old Testament and New Testament? The better question is *who and what* is the predominant figure within the overarching theme? The answer is Jesus. He was prophesied in Genesis as the one to crush the head of the serpent (Gen. 3:15) and continuing up through Revelation as the conquering King (Rev. 19:11-16). Clearly, we see that Jesus Christ is the central message of the Bible. Jesus through the Holy Spirit is the key to unlocking the Bible.

It has been God's plan all along to save mankind through Him. In 2 Timothy 1:9 Paul captures this thought perfectly, *"For God saved us and called us to live a holy life. He did this, not because we deserved it, but because that was his plan from before the beginning of time–to show us his grace through Christ Jesus."*

What is the Biblical Message?

I did a quick Bible word search on the words: love, forgive, grace, sin and judgment. I included the old King James and several modern translations. You will see the translation and the number of times that word is mentioned.

- **Love:** KJV (280), NASB (320), NKJV (335), HCSB (530), NIV (533), and NLT (580).
- **Forgive:** NKJV (47), KJV (48), NASB (54), HCSB (61), NIV (64), and NLT (75).
- **Grace:** NASB (89), NLT (89), NIV (121), HCSB (132), NKJV (141), and KJV (159).
- **Sin:** KJV (388), NASB (394), NKJV (406), HCSB (409), NIV (430), and NLT (468).
- **Judgment:** NIV (139), NASB (174), HCSB (176), NLT (219), NKJV (244), and KJV (285).

Does the Bible point toward love and forgiveness only, or is there more? In the King James translation "Love" is mentioned

280 times and "Sin" 388 times. While we are living in the *"Age of Grace"* (John 1:17), the word "Grace" is referred to 159 times, while *Judgment* is mentioned 285 times in the King James translation and nearly 200 times in each of the modern Bible translations. In the next three sections I want to take a closer look at the three primary characters in the New Testament: Jesus, Peter and Paul. What was their chief message?

Jesus Christ

It is interesting to note that Jesus never used the word *grace*. Yet, he was *"Full of grace and truth"* (John 1:14). Jesus' primary message was about the Kingdom of God. This is summed up in Mark 1:14-15, *"Now after John was put in prison, Jesus came to Galilee, preaching the gospel of the kingdom of God, and saying, 'the time is fulfilled, and the kingdom of God is at hand. Repent, and believe in the gospel.'"* Dr. Mark D. Roberts said, "The phrase 'kingdom of God' appears 53 times in the New Testament Gospels, almost always on the lips of Jesus. The synonymous phrase, 'kingdom of heaven,' appears 32 times in the Gospel of Matthew. Throughout the accounts of Jesus' ministry, he is always talking about the kingdom of God. Many of his parables explain something about this kingdom: it is like a mustard seed, a treasure, a merchant looking for pearls, and a king who gave a banquet. Jesus even defines his purpose in light of the kingdom: *'I must proclaim the good news of the kingdom of God to the other cities also; for I was sent for this purpose'* (Luke 4:43)."

Jesus' primary purpose was to proclaim the gospel (Mark 16:15). Who could argue that Jesus didn't preach exactly what the Father told Him? Jesus said, *"Therefore, whatever I speak, just as the Father has told Me, so I speak"* (John 12:50). Today, we have preachers who purposely leave out the difficult parts of the scripture; the hard truths and principals to make it more appealing. Our purpose should be to proclaim the good news; the whole council of God (Acts 20:27). Have we forgotten the Great Commission; Jesus' final instruction to us? Jesus' final words to preachers and believer should be written on our hearts (Prov. 3:3). Before He ascended He looked out across time, to every preacher and believer and said, *"All authority has been given to Me in heaven and on earth. Go therefore and make disciples of all the nations, baptizing them in the name of the Father and of the Son and of the Holy Spirit, teaching them to observe all things that I have commanded you; and lo, I am with you always, even to the end of the age"* (Matt. 28:18-20). Matthew adds the word, *"Amen"* which means, *let it be so.* It is safe and accurate to say that Jesus expects us to do exactly what He said to do. Unfortunately too many believers have lost sight of this mandate, while others have watered it down to the point of confusion and weakness. There is one more thing that smacks in the face of our lopsided Christianity today. Call it the mission of a lifetime or a mission within the mission. Jesus said, *"You shall be perfect, just as your Father in heaven is perfect"* (Matt. 5:48). Today, many have lowered God's standard to something less than striving for perfection and being like Christ.

The Apostle Peter

Peter was the leader, the primary spokesperson for the disciples. He took the dominate role in the early church. He was a part of Jesus' inner circle along with James and John (Mark 5:37). So, what was Peter's primary message? In his first epistle, 1 Peter, his objective is summed up in the opening verses. The King James (KJV) says, *"Peter, an apostle of Jesus Christ, to the* strangers scattered throughout Pontus, Galatia, Cappadocia, Asia, and Bithynia, elect according to the foreknowledge of God the Father, through sanctification of the Spirit, unto obedience and sprinkling of the blood of Jesus Christ: Grace unto you, and peace, be multiplied" (1 Peter 1:1-2). Easton's Illustrated Dictionary says, "Its object is to confirm its readers in the doctrines they had been already taught." According to Peter we must be sanctified by the Holy Spirit, which leads to living in obedience. Do we confirm and teach all the doctrines Peter warned about?

In Peter's second epistle he makes a reference to his own death (2 Peter 1:14), which some contend, meant that he wrote this book shortly before his death. Speaking to the believer Peter warns about sin and encourages us to have a stronger faith and not be shortsighted. He says, *"For he who lacks these things is shortsighted, even to blindness, and has forgotten that he was cleansed from his old sins. Therefore, brethren, be even more diligent to make your call and election sure, for if you do these things you will never stumble"* (2 Peter 1:9-10). In chapter two Peter deals with false teachers who came from amongst them. This spectacle is a reality in the local church today; we must be on guard. Peter goes on to say, *"Many will follow their destructive ways, because of whom the way of truth will be blasphemed. By covetousness they will exploit you with deceptive words; for a long time their judgment has not been idle, and their destruction does not slumber"* (2 Peter 2:2-3). Few are teaching and warning about the false teachers infiltrating our churches. These deceptive leaders are making slight changes to our Biblical doctrine. If your pastor or teacher hasn't warned you about the sin in your life, get out of that church immediately. Peter warns about shortsightedness, blindness, sins and stumbling. If he did, we should too.

In Chapter three Peter informs us of the reason he wrote his second book. He says, *"Beloved, I now write to you this second epistle (in both of which I stir up your pure minds by way of reminder), that you may be mindful of the words which were spoken before by the holy prophets, and of the commandment of us, the apostles of the Lord and Savior, knowing this first: that scoffers will come in the last days, walking according to their own lusts"* (2 Peter 3:1-3). These disdainers and others like them willingly forget the Word of God (2 Peter 3:5).

When preachers and pastors deliberately fail to teach essential Biblical doctrines we've lost our way. Here's the key point: mockers dwell in the church house, and willingly choose to ignore and reject the Word of God. They are not easy to spot, but we must watch for signs of their actions. To leave out portions of God's Word is to deny the intelligence and absolute power of God. Peter warns us that, not only are these people in the Christian community, but that hell and judgment are coming (2 Peter 3:7). Peter wraps up this book with a "shout out" to the Apostle Paul and the wisdom God had given him. This is another warning about those who are untaught and unstable. They have taken the instructions given by Paul and *"Twist to their own destruction, as they do also the rest of the Scriptures"* (2 Peter 3:16). Peter's main purpose seems to be clear, *"Therefore, since Christ suffered for us in the flesh, arm yourselves also with the same mind, for he who has suffered in the flesh has ceased from sin"* (1 Peter 4:1).

The Apostle Paul

Paul wrote 13 epistles and probably wrote the book of Hebrews. He had a lot more to say than most. Paul may have written the most books, but Luke, who wrote his own gospel and the book of Acts, wrote more overall. My favorite Bible chapter comes from Paul; in Romans chapter 8. My favorite Bible verse also comes from Paul. Romans 8:38-39, *"For I am persuaded that neither death nor life, nor angels nor principalities nor powers, nor things present nor things to come, nor height nor depth, nor any other created thing, shall be able to separate us from the love of God which is in Christ Jesus our Lord."*

Love is the key. Knowing that God loved me was huge. It was liberating when I understood that nothing could come between His great love and me. Through this verse the Holy Spirit helped me understand that I could always count on God, who is love (1 John 4:8). So, I kept the faith and continued moving forward as a young man. As a preacher, I try to preach the Word with love. God's love must consume our local churches. Paul instructs the church in Rome that *"Love must be sincere"* (Rom. 12:9 NIV). So, whether preaching God's grace, God's forgiveness, or God's coming judgment, *"Let all that you do be done with love"* (1 Cor. 16:14). In fact, Paul includes those instructions with *"Watch, stand fast in the faith, be brave, be strong"* (1 Cor. 16:13). It's easy to preach on love, but it takes a brave strong person of faith to preach on sin, hell and judgment. Paul was that man. No matter what we preach we should have the same compassion in our eyes as Jesus did when *"He saw the crowds"* (Matt. 9:36).

One man said, "Paul's writings make me want to be a better Christian." I agree. He was one man chosen by God to enjoy the Christian experience full circle. He went from a persecutor of the early church (Acts 9:1-2), inflicting great suffering, to its greatest champion of suffering (2 Cor. 11:23-28), other than Christ. The New Century (NCV) Dictionary calls him a "Great servant of God." Paul is credited with pointing us to Christ and explaining many of the

Bible's doctrines and principals. Colossians 1:28-29 sums up Paul's central goal, *"Him we preach, warning every man and teaching every man in all wisdom, that we may present every man perfect in Christ Jesus. To this end I also labor, striving according to His working which works in me mightily."*

One of the great tragedies about Christianity today, is that few strive for the perfection Jesus spoke about. Paul is only echoing Jesus' call to be perfect (Matt. 5:48). Where has the echo gone? Does it reverberate in our local churches? Sadly, many are teaching believers to settle for mediocrity. There is nothing mediocre about Jesus. While perfection cannot be attained on earth, it must be the goal. Paul taught, *"If anyone is in Christ, he is a new creation; old things have passed away; behold, all things have become new"* (2 Cor. 5:17). The end-time church will be

> *"Today, many Christians talk about Jesus' walk, rather than walk like Jesus talked." -DLF*

largely lazy and asleep. Some have already rewritten this verse to say, "If anyone is in Christ, he is a new creation; some old things are okay; because of grace, some things are okay." As a new creation in Christ we must have a vital union with Christ.

How we live and what we do is central to Paul's overall message to the church. In Colossians 2:6-7 Paul says, *"As you have therefore received Christ Jesus the Lord, so walk in Him, rooted and built up in Him and established in the faith, as you have been taught, abounding in it with thanksgiving."* Paul makes it clear what should happen after receiving Christ. What does it mean to be rooted in Christ? Built up in Jesus? Established in the faith? Paul's message to the first century church is the same for us today. His message centers on how we live for Christ. Ephesians 5:1-20 is a further example of Paul's intentions. Take some time to read it. Verse 15 in the

New International Version (NIV) says, *"Be very careful, then, how you live--not as unwise but as wise."* Where is our wisdom today? Even Jesus warned, in the last days, unwise believers will be left behind (Matt. 25). Being rooted, built up, established, and carefully walking with Christ takes a daily commitment. It means making a decision not to compromise Biblical principles for anything or anyone. Sadly, many are promoting the philosophy that once a person gets saved they can basically live a life in the grey areas. Like some *gap theorist*, they live in-between specific verses that give credence to their thinking. Make no mistake about it, how we live in God's Kingdom matters.

Innocent of Man's Blood

At the end of it all Paul made an astounding claim, *"I am innocent of man's blood"* (Acts 20:26). Paul worked hard at this innocence, we should too. Matthew Henry's Concise Commentary says, "He was a truly Christian, evangelical preacher; he did not preach notions or doubtful matters; nor affairs of state or the civil government; but he preached faith and repentance." The Bible and Jesus is our source of all wisdom (1 Cor. 1:30). It must guide our words and ways. If we don't wake up and use all of it, we are guilty of a great misuse of our divinely called believers.

To be innocent of man's blood we must preach and teach the totality of God's Word. Only from a birds-eye view can we see God's divine plan throughout scripture. Only with a magnifying glass can we rightly understand and interpret the details of the Word. What we see, interpret and deliver matters. God has placed us in the Body of Christ to minister to others. Like Paul, can each of us say "There is not going to be any blood on my hands?"

Chapter 8 – Who's On the Lord's Side?

"A debate is a conflict which clarifies a position. A dialogue is a conversation which compromises a position." – U.S. Representative John Ashbrook

Two kinds of people

Not only are there two gates and two roads, but there are two kinds of people. There are those who are ready and those who are not ready. I believe the Bible is calling spiritual leaders and others appointed by the Lord to define the difference. Someone must speak out about the difference between those who are truly in the game, and those who are watching from the sidelines. In today's Christian culture it is becoming much more difficult to distinguish the difference between the two groups. It was Jesus who called for a separation, *"His own special people"* (1 Pet. 2:9). The following is a list of the two kinds of people in our world:

- **Those who are for Christ and those who are against Him –** Too many are giving Jesus less than all. There are over 100 verses in the New Testament containing both the words: "Jesus" and "All." Luke 11:23 says, *"He who is not with Me is against Me, and he who does not gather with Me scatters."* The choice is clear: People are either for Him, or fighting against Him.

- **Those who believe Jesus is the <u>only</u> way and those who don't** – This is a massive problem today. *USA Today* reporting in an unbelievable new survey that 52 percent of American Christians believe that eternal life is not exclusively for those who accept Jesus Christ as their savior. A Pew Research Center's Forum on Religion & Public Life found that 57 percent of evangelical Christians in America believe that "many religions can lead to eternal life". The fact is, to believe there are many ways, is calling Jesus a liar." In John 14:6 Jesus said, *"I am the way, the truth, and the life. No one comes to the Father except through Me."*

- **Those who believe in God's Son and those who don't** – Too many today believe OF HIM and not IN HIM. These have head knowledge and don't know the Son of God, Jesus Christ intimately. Some forget, *"Even the demons believe and shutter"* (James 2:19). No one expects a demon to be in heaven. John 3:15 (KJV) says, *"Whosoever believeth in him should not perish, but have eternal life."*

- **Those who are rejected by Jesus and those who are accepted** – Today there are two end-time churches side by side (Rev. 3:7-22). The Philadelphian believers love and follow God's Word with passion. The Laodicean believers live a Luke-warm life, rejecting the Word of God. This makes God sick. As a stomach rejects bad food, these so-called believers are also rejected (Heb. 6:4-8). Regarding this unfaithful group of people Jesus said, *"I know your works, that you are neither cold nor hot. I could wish you were cold or hot. So then, because you are lukewarm, and neither cold nor hot, I will vomit you out of my mouth"* (Rev. 3:15-16).

- **Those who serve Him and those who don't** – Matthew 6:24 *"No one can serve two masters; for either he will hate the one and love the other, or else he will be loyal to the one and despise the other."* Divided service to the God of Scripture is impossible. The Jewish people have a saying related to this kind of service; "We have not found that, 'any man is fit for two tables.'" They also say, "It is not proper for one man to have two governments."

- **Those who accept the entire Bible as truth and those who don't** – It seems the smarter mankind gets, the further from the truth we become. The Word of God is a believers foundation; whether an individual or a nation. Erode the foundation and the righteous will suffer (Ps. 11:3). As He was praying to the Father for His disciples, Jesus declared, *"Your word is truth"* (John 17:17). Today, the Bible is under attack both inside and outside the church. Christianity is being destroyed from within because many have forgotten that "All" the Bible, every word, is truth. Those who take bits and pieces, or parts out of the Word are themselves deceived. The Bible says, *"All scripture is inspired"* (2 Tim. 3:16).

- **Those who are condemned and those who are not** – God is the judge (Ps. 7:11). All of us are destined to die in our sins. After all, *"The wages of sin is death"* (Rom. 6:23). The enemy of our soul is the *"Accuser"* (Rev. 12:10), and day and night works against us (Job 1:9-11). Condemnation is for those who have rejected the blood of Jesus. When the judge sees the blood covering the sin, *"There is therefore no condemnation for those in Christ Jesus"* (Rom. 8:1). The key is to *"Walk not after the flesh, but after the Spirit"* (Rom. 8:1).

- **Those who believe in ONE GOD and those who believe in many** – Those who adhere to the existence of other gods are wrong biblically. James 2:19 says, *"You believe that there is one God. You do well. Even the demons believe–and tremble!"* There is only one true living God and His Son Jesus Christ (Jer. 10:10; John 17:3).

- **Those who belong to God and those who don't** – Everyone wants to belong to someone, or something. Either you belong to God and *"Were bought at a price"* (1 Cor. 6:19-20), or you belong to *"Your father the devil"* (John 8:44). It is the difference between the *"Spirit of truth or the spirit of deception"* (1 John 4:6). The world is full of those who do not *"Acknowledge the truth about Jesus, that person is not from God"* (1 John 4:3).

- **Those who confess Christ and those who deny Christ** – When Peter denied Christ three times he ended up weeping bitterly (Luke 22:62-64), but was profoundly sorry for his actions. Today, far too many boldly deny Christ and put themselves in a very dangerous place. Sadly, too many believers deny Christ by their lifestyle. In Matthew 10:32-33 Jesus warns, *"Whoever confesses Me before men, him I will also confess before My Father who is in heaven. But whoever denies Me before men, him I will also deny before My Father who is in heaven."*

- **Those on the right and those on the left** – Hell will be full of those whom refused to deal with sin. While the Bible says, *"All have sinned"* (Rom. 3:23), some don't accept this. God has always separated the sinner from the righteous. From Noah to Sodom and Gomorrah, and to the end of the age when, *"The angels will come forth, separate the* *wicked from among the just, and cast them into the furnace of fire"* (Matthew 13:49). One day, some will go to the right (the sheep) and others to the left (the goats). Sadly, those on His left will hear the most horrify words ever said to anyone, *"Depart from me, you cursed, into the everlasting fire prepared for the devil and his angels"* (Matt. 25:31-46).

- **Those who will be raptured and those who won't** – Many believe the next prophetic event on God's calendar will be the rapture of the church (1 Thess. 4:16-17). Matthew 25 is a controversial passage because the ten virgins are split into two groups; five wise and five foolish. In the Greek, virgin *(parthenos)* means virgin, not bridesmaid. While some contend the foolish virgins were unbelievers, 2 Corinthians 11:2 compares virgins to believers, calling us *"A chaste virgin to Christ."* As the end approaches, we are instructed to *"Watch therefore, for you do not know what hour your Lord is coming"* (Matt. 24:42). The fact remains, *"Two men will be in the field: one will be taken and the other left. Two women will be grinding at the mill: one will be taken and the other left"* (Matt. 24:40-41). Regardless of whether these verses pertain to the rapture of not, it appears, when the trumpet sounds, some will be left behind to face the wrath of God.

The People of God have changed

In the New Living Testament (NLT), Hebrews 13:17 is a summons to all believers. The writer says, *"Obey your spiritual leaders, and do what they say. Their work is to watch over your souls, and they are accountable to God."* There are two kinds of people represented in this scripture verse. First, are the believers who attend the local church. They are given a scriptural command, a serious mandate of obedience. While obedience is the required for service in the Kingdom of God, the specific command to *obey* is often ignored. There is a difference between a paid staff member and a volunteer. It's easy to ask the paid staff to follower orders, because their job is on the line. They we're brought on to help the leader and thus required to follow. What about the lay leaders who are volunteers? I admit, as a pastor I've never told a person in the church, "Do what I say." Yet, the people of God are required to listen, obey and do what is asked of them. Obedience to the Lord is a fading facet of the local church. People don't faithfully follow their leaders anymore.

The second group are the church leaders; the spiritual leadership of the local church. The passage puts great responsibility on them; to watch souls, and give an account. The individual soul is the ultimate issue. Jesus said, *"For what will it profit a man if he gains the whole world, and loses his own soul?"* (Luke 8:36). For spiritual leaders to mess around with the souls of man; which is a regular occurrence today, is dangerous business. A soul is the most precious treasure in God's Kingdom. Therefore, accountability is demanded and expected; requiring a face to face with the soul-maker someday.

Jesus goes on to say in Luke 8:37, *"What will a man give in exchange for his soul?"* The Bible Knowledge Commentary answers the question. "Nothing, because having *gained the world* he has in the end irrevocably lost eternal life with God, with nothing to compensate for it." We have reached a critical place in American culture; the soul is no longer the focus. Everything has changed. US Representative John Ashbrook said, "A debate is a conflict which clarifies a position. A dialogue is a conversation which compromises a position." Christians in America are no longer in a debate, but a conversation. We've gone from conflict to compromise. In other words, our position in the culture has shifted.

The Bible as truth has all but been eliminated from our society. Therefore, the soul and eternal life is off of the average person's radar. This has greatly affected the local church as well. The average believers' commitment to the leadership inside church walls has changed. Amazingly, people are willing trade their souls for cheap thrills and temporary things. Fading are the days of commitment in the local church. People drift in and out; often with a growing sense that says, "What can you do for me" not, "What can I do to serve." The word obey has been thrown out like yesterday's newspaper. Overall, the people of God, in America have changed their minds about commitment. Christian blogger, Arsenio A. Lembert Jr. says it like this: "Americanized Christianity brings me to borderline nausea... the denominationalism, and the all-around lukewarm nature of the "Church" is disheartening and concerning. These days, it seems you have to qualify your "Christianity" because saying "I'm a Christian" is really indicative of nothing."

Time is running out

Who gave believers the permission to change? When did we stop focusing on the early church and the way Jesus set things up? Methods can change but not the message. A "Paradigm Shift" is another way to explain this sad phenomenon happening today. In the business world, according to *Investopeida.com*, "...Paradigm shifts can require that entire departments be eliminated or created in some cases, and millions or even billions of dollars of new equipment purchased while the old equipment is sold or recycled. Paradigm shifts have become much more frequent in the past hundred years, as the industrial revolution has transformed many social and industrial processes. This process is likely to become even more commonplace in the future as our rate of technological advancement increases." Can you see the parallels? New ways, other than Biblical are invented to explain life and creation. The standard Christ and the early church set is being recycled into something else. The transformation of our Christian culture is a new revolution. As newspapers are being replaced by the internet, the Word of God is being exchanged with self-help books and sermons. Likewise, fellowship in the local church is being replaced by social media and the neighborhood Starbucks. Like all things, this new paradigm shift will reach its end. One day, the Lord will hear the cry of those slain for their faith. Their blood will scream out, *"How long, O Lord, holy and true, until You judge and avenge our blood on those who dwell on the earth?"* (Rev. 6:10).

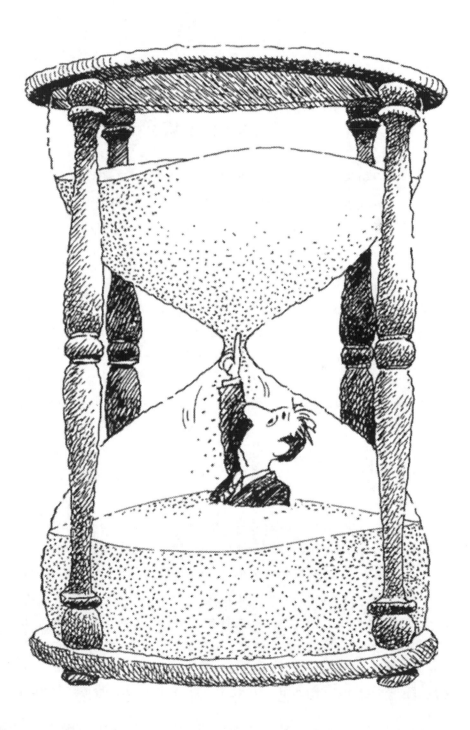

Chapter 9 – A Strong Warning

"False doctrine has never ceased to be the plague of Christendom for the last twenty-one centuries" –Dr. Walter Martin

The Warning is clear

Peter warned of the day when false teaches and prophets will infiltrate the church. *"But there were also false prophets among the people, even as there will be false teachers among you, who will secretly bring in destructive heresies, even denying the Lord who bought them, and bring on themselves swift destruction"* (2 Peter 2:1). That day has come, for they live among us in droves. Some of them are willfully false and some are mere victims of ignorance. They have been occupying the pews for years and their subtle lies and deceptions have taken root. They are growing in their stance against those who preach and teach the whole Gospel and the harder truths? They have distorted the true message and purpose of the local church; which is to win the lost. They work harder at not offending people, rather than giving them the truth of God in the spirit of love. Something is terribly wrong when pastors and churches decide to no longer speak publically about social issues. My biggest question to them is; what are you going to do when a topic you reject or that the politically correct culture deems wrong, comes up in the

Biblical text. To preach or not to preach, that is the question. What would a true believer do? What would a false believer and teacher do? A false teacher would  simply ignore it. What does that say about them? If you won't preach publically about homosexuality, are you going to ignore those portions of scripture? Did the Father make a mistake putting social issues in His Word? Is only some of scripture relevant for today? The plain truth is, someday you will have to speak to these and other social issues. This approach to preaching the gospel of Christ in view of these social issues is perplexing. Here is what one major churches approach is to this specific issue.

Here are their comments from ChristianPost.com: "We have a stance on love, and we have a conversation on everything else." Hillsong New York City Pastor Carl Lentz has made it clear that he will not take a public stance on social issues like homosexuality because, as he said during media appearances, that is not the example Jesus Christ models in the Bible. When asked during an interview with Katie Couric on her self-titled daytime show if he felt that he had a moral imperative to speak publicly about "some of these more controversial issues," Lentz said, "No, because we try to be like Jesus." There are several examples of Jesus speaking out publically about the social issues of His day: (1) the church (God's house), when He threw out the money changers (Matt. 21:12-13). (2) Money, when He facing the rich young ruler (Mark 10:17-27).

(3) Racism, when He met the woman at the well (John 4:1-42). (4) Suffering people, when He dealt with the man in the region of the Gadarenes (Luke 8:26-39). (5) Government, when He was confronted on paying taxes (Mark 12:13-17). (6) Religion, when He spoke to the religious leaders (Matt. 23:1-39). Probably the greatest example was Jesus' most famous teaching, The Sermon on the Mount in Matthew chapters 5-7. This open air message is a smorgasbord of teachings on social issues like: Anger, murder, adultery, divorce, those who treat you wrongly, giving to the poor, false prophets, the law and more. Jesus covered topics like the poor (Matt. 19:21; Luke 4:18-19), justice (Luke 18:1-8), authority (Mark 10:42-45), and being a good person (Luke 10:30-37). If Jesus spoke openly about these issues and others, why should it be any different today?

> A pastor or preacher should never keep the flock from Biblical doctrine or truths. If he or she does...run!

When Jesus returns the consummation of all the remaining Biblical prophecies will happen quickly. Those false prophets and misguided spiritual leaders will be identified. I believe most will repent and cry out to the Lord as Peter did after his denial. For many it will be too late. The Apostle Peter makes it clear these false leaders will suffer swift destruction. In 2 Peter 2:21 he said, *"For it would have been better for them not to have known the way of righteousness, than having known it, to turn from the holy commandment delivered to them."* The time has come to warn all believers and those who claim to be Christians. What is the warning? The prophet Haggai, speaking for the Lord said, *"Consider your ways!"* (Haggai 1:7). Those who misinterpret the scriptures will say that warning people of judgment is based on fear. They can't be further from the truth. God is warning His people that judgment is coming, and He does everything based on love. Pay close attention to the spiritual leaders in your life. If they are, in anyway, negating the Word of God, they are hurting the Body of Christ. They may be good people, but they might be deceived. They might be doing great things for God, but don't let their good works keep you from Biblical doctrine and truth.

The Message Bible warns us in Hosea 4:6, *"My people are ruined because they don't know what's right or true. Because you've turned your back on knowledge, I've turned my back on you priests. Because you refuse to recognize the revelation of God, I'm no longer recognizing your children."* Notice three things and apply them to our day: (1) God's people are ruined because they don't know what is right or true. (2) God's people have rejected knowledge, which comes from God's Word, the Bible. (3) God appears to hold the priests (spiritual leaders) responsible and rejects them. The Life Application Bible Notes says, "God accused the religious leaders of keeping the people from knowing him (destroyed from lack of knowledge). They were supposed to be spiritual leaders, but they had become leaders in wrongdoing." (4) The spiritual leaders did not see the revelation of God. The Bible Exposition Commentary on the Old Testament adds, "Worldly and ignorant spiritual leaders produce worldly and ignorant people, and this brings destruction to the land." (5) The lack of leadership ultimately hurts the children and the generations to come.

As the Lord has warned us in the past, He is warning us today. The Bible is packed-full of warnings. There are several scriptures that compel us to watch and warn the people that danger and destruction are coming. Here are a few to soak up:

- **A flood is coming** - Genesis 6:9-22
- **The city is about to be destroyed** – Genesis 19:1-29
- **The death angel is coming** – Exodus 12:1-28
- **The nation will be exiled** – 2 Kings 25:1-30
- **A house or city that rejects the Message of Christ** – Matthew 10:14-15
- **Those who will not believe** – Jude 1:5-8
- **It will be like the days of Noah** – Matthew 24:37-39
- **It will be like the days of Lot** – Luke 17:28-32
- **The rapture is coming** – 1 Thessalonians 4:16-17; 1 Corinthians 15:52
- **Some will be left behind** – Luke 17:34-36; Matthew 25:1-13
- **The antichrist will come** – Revelation 13:11-18
- **The Tribulation is coming** – Daniel 9:24-27; Joel 1:15; 1 Thessalonians 5:2
- **The mark of the beast** – Revelation 13:16-18; 20:4
- **The Tribulation begins with a covenant with Israel** – Daniel 9:27
- **The Second Coming of Christ** – Matthew 24:30-31
- **One day evil will be destroyed** – 2 Thessalonians 2:8
- **The judgment seat of Christ** – 2 Corinthians 5:10
- **The Great White Throne judgment** – Revelation 20:11-15
- **Called to be watchman** – Ezekiel 3:16-17 *"Now it came to pass at the end of seven days that the word of the Lord came to me, saying, "Son of man, I have made you a watchman for the house of Israel; therefore hear a word from My mouth, and give them warning from Me."*
- **Warn the wicked** – Ezekiel 33:7-9 *"So you, son of man: I have made you a watchman for the house of Israel; therefore you shall hear a word from My mouth and warn them for Me.*

When I say to the wicked, 'O wicked man, you shall surely die!' and you do not speak to warn the wicked from his way, that wicked man shall die in his iniquity; but his blood I will require at your hand. Nevertheless if you warn the wicked to turn from his way, and he does not turn from his way, he shall die in his iniquity; but you have delivered your soul."

- **The Day of the Lord is coming** – Joel 2:1 *"Blow the trumpet in Zion, And sound an alarm in My holy mountain! Let all the inhabitants of the land tremble; For the day of the Lord is coming, For it is at hand."*

A Warning for America

A few years ago I was meeting with several pastors in my area. We began to discuss different issues facing the churches we pastor. Assuming everyone thought as I did about why the Body of Christ struggled, I spoke about strongholds. I couldn't believe the push-back I received. One pastor said, "There's nothing wrong with the church...the local church is fine." Another said, "There were no demonic forces over our city." It's hard to imagine that so many don't see the plight of the local churches, and the Body of Christ in America. Satan is succeeding at pulling the wool over the eyes of many, even in the local churches. Do you watch the news? Few would argue that America is weaker today in her moral standing. Many don't see the dangers facing us. Are we better off? I don't think so. In fact, we are in major trouble due to the fact that we have lost our moral compass. Back in 1965 the prophetic words of ABC radio commentator Paul Harvey are alarming. During his broadcast on April 3, 1965, he pinpointed the future of the nation. Paul Harvey gave this nation a strong warning.

IF I WERE THE DEVIL

If I were the devil...if I were the Prince of Darkness, I'd want to engulf the whole world in darkness. And I'd have a third of its real estate, and four-fifths of its population, but I wouldn't be happy until I had seized the ripest apple on the tree — Thee. So, I'd set about however necessary to take over the United States. I'd subvert the churches first — I'd begin with a campaign of whispers. With the wisdom of a serpent, I would whisper to you as I whispered to Eve: 'Do as you please.' "To the young, I would whisper that 'The Bible is a myth.' I would convince them that man created God instead of the other way around. I would confide that what's bad is good, and what's good is 'square.' And the old, I would teach to pray, after me, 'Our Father, which art in Washington...' "And then I'd get organized. I'd educate authors in how to make lurid literature exciting, so that anything else would appear dull and uninteresting. I'd threaten TV with dirtier movies and vice versa. I'd pedal narcotics to whom I could. I'd sell alcohol to ladies and gentlemen of distinction. I'd tranquilize the rest with pills. "If I were the devil I'd soon have families that war with themselves, churches at war with themselves, and nations at war with themselves; until each in its turn was consumed. And with promises of higher ratings I'd have mesmerizing media fanning the flames. If I were the devil I would encourage schools to refine young intellects, but neglect to discipline emotions — just let those run wild, until before you knew it, you'd have to have drug sniffing dogs and metal detectors at every schoolhouse door. "Within a decade I'd have prisons overflowing, I'd have judges promoting pornography — soon I could evict God from the courthouse, then from the schoolhouse, and then from the houses of Congress. And in His own churches I would substitute psychology for religion, and deify science. I would lure priests and pastors into misusing boys and girls, and church money. If I were the devil I'd make the symbols of Easter an egg and the symbol of Christmas a bottle. "If I were the devil I'd take from those who have, and give to those who wanted until I had killed the incentive of the ambitious. And what do you bet? I couldn't get whole states to promote gambling as thee way to get rich? I would caution against extremes and hard work, in Patriotism, in moral conduct. I would convince the young that marriage is old-fashioned, that swinging is more fun, that what you see on TV is the way to be. And thus I could undress you in public, and I could lure you into bed with diseases for which there is no cure. In other words, if I were the devil I'd just keep right on doing on what he's doing. Paul Harvey, good day."

Consider yourself warned. I don't believe God is going to allow things to continue as they are. The sins of America have filled the cup. Pastor and prophetic voice for America, David Wilkerson said, "The church in America is far from what God has envisioned it to be." Something has to give. God doesn't tolerate evil forever. Just ahead, around the corner for all of us in America is one of four things: A final outpouring of God's Spirit, the rapture of the church, economic collapse, or the Tribulation hour. Which one is coming first, and in what order is unknown to us. Nevertheless, soon something awesome is coming upon America and the world.

True believers

If you've read this far, you have heard the truth I proclaim to you. In Joel 3:9 it says, *"Proclaim this among the nations: 'Prepare for war! Wake up the mighty men, Let all the men of war draw near, Let them come up.'"* Imagine the early Americans who were unsure what was coming next. Like them, we must rise up and take up arms and prepare for what is coming. Patrick Henry said, "The battle is not to the strong, but to the vigilant, the active, and the brave." So, let us be brave, vigilant, and active. We don't have to be strong, that is God's responsibility. The Apostle Paul reminds us, *"When I am weak, then I am strong"* (2 Cor. 12:10). More than anything else let us be true believers. Make the following your declaration:

A true believer

I have made my choice (Josh. 24:15). I know what I believe (2 Tim. 1:12). Nobody can take away what Jesus has done for me (Luke 8:39). I will work hard to please God (Gal. 1:10). I am a soldier in the army of the Lord (2 Tim. 2:3-4). When He speaks I listen (Deut. 5:24). When

He leads, I follow (Luke 9:57). He is the real Commander in Chief (Joel 2:11). I'm ready to step into the ring and fight (1 Tim. 6:12). My battle is not against people (Eph. 6:12), but against the devil (James 4:7). I will love others no matter what they have done (John 13:35). The Lord is with me (Ps. 118:6). I have a promise from God to be successful and win (Ps. 60:12). I am ready to die in the arena (Acts 21:13). When the enemy roars, I will not flinch (1 Pet. 5:8). When the giants attack, with God, I will have the victory (1 Sam. 17:48-51). I no-longer care about this world (1 John 2:15). I don't care what the politically correct crowd might say (Gal. 1:10), I have my orders from the Master (Mk. 16:15). His Word is truth (John 17:17), my delight (Jer. 15:16), and the power I need (Rom. 1:16). The Bible will be the love of my life (Ps. 119:97). His Word will be a fire in my bones (Jer. 20:9). I will not be ashamed of the gospel (Rom. 1:16). I will preach it, all of it with passion (2 Tim. 4:2). I am a big time, radical believer in Jesus Christ (Acts 16:31). I am a sold out committed follower (Luke 9:23). I will give until there is nothing left (Mark 12:44). I will serve until the job is done (Eph. 6:7). I will do whatever the Master asks (John 14:23). I will live my life for Christ (Phil. 1:21). The world will know that I love Jesus with all my heart (Matt. 22:37). I will never cease to be a true believer.

Chapter 10 – The Fork in the Road

*"Nothing or nobody is worth going
to hell over"* –Roger Brown

Put on your turn signal

After Jesus was tempted by the Devil in the wilderness He began His Galilean ministry. *"From that time Jesus began to preach and say, 'Repent, for the kingdom of heaven is at hand'"* (Matt. 4:17). We know that it is impossible for anyone to be saved without repentance (Acts 2:38). Repentance is "making a U-Turn for Christ" and going in the other direction. A 180 is the calling of every lost person. Regrettably, too many will miss it. Their hearts and minds will be busy with the things of this world. In fact, the major difference between those heading down the broad road and those who see the narrow gate is what Jesus said to Peter in Matthew 16:23 *"Get behind Me, Satan! You are an offense to Me, for you are not mindful of the things of God, but the things of men."* Like the turn signal in every automobile, salvation is within reach. The lost who fail to use it will ultimately crash and burn. We cannot forget those who apostatize from the faith (2 Thess. 2). They too need to reach for the turn signal and stop merely going through the motions of Christianity. They are missing divine detours and are in danger of God's judgment.

Seeing the parting of the road

One day on a motorcycle riding trip I came to a fork in the road. I stopped because I didn't see which way the team went. I sat there for a moment imagining the worst case scenarios. On a previous trip I rode past a coyote. So, I just knew it must be watching me. I looked around imagining it pouncing on me. I felt alone and began to panic. Then I saw it off to the left. For confirmation I leaned in, and  squinting my eyes. Then after a quick sigh of relief, I followed the tire tracks and eventually caught up to them. God is all about choices. In fact, free-will comes with plenty of them. It's like the king of Babylon, all of us will stand *"At the parting of the road"* (Ezekiel 21:21).

This parting is called, "A fork in the road." It's a place where the path splits into choices. In view of our Heavenly Father, one path, especially the wrong one can end in death. The Bible is our guide. As Jesus said, *"Follow me"* to the disciples, the Bible announces the same to us today. God's fork in the road is the most serious choice. The fork in the road makes one consider the joy of heaven or the agony of hell. As the narrow road has its choices, so does the broad road. In the midst of every choice, God has a plan for us all. For *"This gospel of the kingdom will be preached in all the world as a witness to all the nations, and then the end will come"* (Matt. 24:14). In that moment of decision, there are two paths: the first choice is a narrow way, "*A highway of holiness*" (Isa. 35:8). The second path is a wide path which "*Is the way that leads to destruction*" (Matt. 7:13-14). The fork in the road is a choice between God's way or the devil's; the truth of God or a lie.

All of us can live for God and make the right choice to get off the wrong road. Have you heard of Ivan Moiseyev? He was a fearless young man whose boldness for Christ made him a testimony to millions of believers around the world. Ivan Moiseyev, known as Vanya was a soldier in the Soviet Red Arm. He shined in the dark shadows of Soviet atheism. For two years he suffered for Christ by trial and torture. Like Abraham "*He did not waver at the promise of God through unbelief, but was strengthened in faith, giving glory to God*" (Rom. 4:20). Vanya had the courage to lovingly stand up to his commanders. On one occasion, after several attempt to rehabilitate and give him the opportunity to change his views and reform back to Red Army ways, Vanya said, "*Comrade commissar, the Bible teaches believers to obey the authorities placed over them. It is my deep desire to do this. But the Bible further teaches us that our supreme Master is God. His authority demands from us complete obedience and commitment. I beg of you to understand that I have two sets of loyalties--loyalty to the state and loyalty to God. If I am commanded to do something that would cause me to disobey God, then I am obligated to put my loyalty to Him first.*"

It's time to BELIEVE

There is hope for this world. I would like to end this book by encouraging you to stand up and live a life with passion for Christ. There is no middle ground. I'm not talking about religious rules, or being under the law. I'm speaking about what is written and has never changed, "*He who called you is holy, you also be holy in* all your conduct, because it is written, 'Be holy, for I am holy.'" (1 Pet. 1:15-16). This is what it means to be a Christian, someone who follows hard after Jesus, *"Who has saved us and called us with a holy calling, not according to our works, but according to His own purpose and grace which was given to us in Christ Jesus before time began"* (2 Tim. 1:9). We must change the way we live and embrace the Word of God. It's not a matter of committing one act; which is something God forgives. It is about a choice to live on the broad road; which is embracing a lifestyle apart from Jesus. We must turn, change and repent or it will bring condemnation. We have a mandate to change our ways, and help others do the same. Dr. Martin Luther King Jr. said, "Take the first step in faith. You don't have to see the whole staircase, just the take the first step." My friends, it's time to B.E.L.I.E.V.E.:

Believe only in Jesus Christ, the Word of God; which is truth – *"Most assuredly, I say to you, he who hears My word and believes in Him who sent Me has everlasting life, and shall not come into judgment, but has passed from death into life"* (John 5:24).

Eternal Damnation is at stake – *"And they were judged, each one according to his works. Then Death and Hades were cast into the lake of fire. This is the second death. And anyone not found written in the Book of Life was cast into the lake of fire"* (Revelation 20:13-15).

Love God's people no matter what road they're on – *"But the end of all things is at hand; therefore be serious and watchful in your prayers. And above all things have fervent* love for one another, for *"love will cover a multitude of sins"* (1 Peter 4:7-8).

Invite all people to know Jesus Christ personally – *"If you confess with your mouth the Lord Jesus and believe in your heart that God has raised Him from the dead, you will be saved. For with the heart one believes unto righteousness, and with the mouth confession is made unto salvation"* (Romans 10:9-10).

Everlasting Life is a stake – *"For our citizenship is in heaven, from which we also eagerly wait for the Savior, the Lord Jesus Christ, who will transform our lowly body that it may be conformed to His glorious body"* (Philippians 3:20-21).

Voice the truth, which is the Word of God, regardless of what the culture says – *"But sanctify the Lord God in your hearts, and always be ready to give a defense to everyone who asks you a reason for the hope that is in you, with meekness and fear; having a good conscience, that when they defame you as evildoers, those who revile your good conduct in Christ may be ashamed. For it is better, if it is the will of God, to suffer for doing good than for doing evil"* (1 Peter 3:15-17).

Energize those around you to live for Jesus with passion – *"Obey in all things your masters according to the flesh, not with eyeservice, as men-pleasers, but in sincerity of heart, fearing God. And whatever you do, do it heartily, as to the Lord and not to men, knowing that from the Lord you will* receive the reward of the inheritance; for you serve the Lord Christ" (Colossians 3:22-24).

John 3:18 (my parenthesis added)
"He who believes in Him is not condemned (The Narrow Road); but he who does not believe is condemned already (The Broad Road...the 8-Land Highway)"

Chapter 11 – God Has a Plan for You

"For I, the Son of Man, must die since it is
part of God's plan" -Luke 22:22 (NLT)

Christian people have always declared, "God has a plan." The Bible backs them up. God has a plan for the nation of Israel, *"But they do not know the thoughts of the LORD; they do not understand his plan"* (Micah 4:12 NIV). God has a plan to save mankind through Christ who, *"Though He was delivered up according to God's determined plan and foreknowledge, you used lawless people to nail Him to a cross and kill Him"* (Acts 2:23 HCSB). God has a plan for believers *"Because we are united with Christ, we have received an inheritance from God, for he chose us in advance, and he makes everything work out according to his plan"* (Eph. 1:11 NLT).

God's plan for you is real. It is the one thing you can count on. It stretches from creating the massive universe to the tiniest atom in your body. God's plan began with a command, *"Let there be light"* (Gen. 1:3). Likewise, God's plan for you begins with a command, *"Whoever calls on the name of the Lord Shall be saved"* (Acts 2:21). As God's awesome plan began with words, so must your journey.

To understand God's plan for you, I've put together a simple acrostic. It will show you how much God wants to know you personally. A real-life relationship with His Son Jesus Christ is God's plan for all. At the end of this chapter there is a simple prayer, a guideline for you to use. The Bible tells us that a simple prayer of *"Confession is made unto salvation"* (Rom. 10:10). The creator made it simple to begin your relationship with the Father; believe in Jesus the Son and confess your mistakes. Whether your prayer is for the first time, or one of rededication to the Lord, I applaud your choice. You are making the greatest decision in your life. Your decision today will help you by-pass the broad road, finding the narrow gate, the narrow road, and eternal life. Your decision to accept Christ effects heaven itself (Luke 15:7).

God's P.L.A.N. for You

P – You need a **PLACE** to go. Jesus assured us, *"I go to prepare a place for you"* (John 14:2). The place He is referring to is heaven, where the Father is. Something powerful happens when you believe, by faith in Jesus. The Bible says it like this, *"Most assuredly, I say to you, he who hears My word and believes in Him who sent Me has everlasting life, and shall not come into judgment, but has passed from death into life"* (John 5:24).

> **God's Promise:** To prepare a wonderful, beautiful place for you to go someday.

<u>L</u> – You need to be **LOVED**. No one can love you like God does. John 3:16 says, *"For God so loved the world that He gave His only begotten Son, that whoever believes in Him should not perish but have everlasting life."* Nothing can separate you from His love (Rom. 8:38). God's greatest desire is a realtionship with you here on earth and in heaven. Jesus said, *"Behold, I stand at the door and knock. If anyone hears My voice and opens the door, I will come in to him and dine with him, and he with Me. To him who overcomes I will grant to sit with Me on My throne, as I also overcame and sat down with My Father on His throne"* (Rev. 3:20-21).

God's Promise: A special relationship with
you through Jesus Christ His Son.

<u>A</u> - You need an **ANTIDOTE** for sin. There is a poison flowing though mankind, called sin. Sin is the poison working through your body to destroy you and your future. The Bible says, *"All have sinned and fall short of God's glory"* (Rom. 3:23). If sin were a job, the wages would be death (Romans 6:23). Jesus and His love is the antidote for the sin in your life. *"Love will cover a multitude of sins"* (1 Peter 4:7-8).

God's Promise: To forgive all your sins
and help you through this life.

<u>N</u> - You need a savior **NOW**. The Bible says, *"Today is the day for salvation"* (2 Cor. 6:2). God's plan for you is real and He desires that it starts now, today. You're need for a Savior is real. That is why Jesus came to the earth, *"To seek and to save what was lost"* (Luke 19:10). Being saved begins with

a relationship and is the greatest thing in the world. By making Jesus your Lord and Savior He will forgive your past, transform your present, and make your future secure. Yes, God has a tremendous plan for you; a plan effecting your past, present and especially your future. Long ago God made this declaration to you: *"I know the plans I have for you, plans to prosper you and not to harm you, plans to give you hope and a future"* (Jer. 29:11 ₙᵢᵥ).

> **God's Promise:** To be your Savior. To give you
> freedom from the past, help for the present
> and the most amazing future in heaven.

Steps to knowing Jesus as your Savior

The Bible says, *"If you confess with your mouth the Lord Jesus and believe in your heart that God has raised Him from the dead, you will be saved. For with the heart one believes unto righteousness, and with the mouth confession is made unto salvation"* (Romans 10:9-10). A relationship with Jesus (knowing Him) is very simple to begin. **Step one** – Pray a prayer of confession, with your mouth. Confessing your sins to the Lord is very important because Jesus died for your sins. **Step two** – Believe in your heart (by faith) in Jesus Christ and what He accomplished for you. The Bible proves that He lived, died and rose again. You might not understand everything, but you can accept it by faith. The Bible declares, *"He who believes in the Son has everlasting life"* (John 3:36). **Step three** – Invite Jesus into your heart and life with a simple conversation (prayer). There is not a specific Biblical formula to pray. Prayer in its simplest form is just talking with God. Use the simple guide below as you talk to the Father. Joel 2:32 says, *"It shall come to pass that whoever calls on the name of the Lord Shall be saved."*

A Simple Prayer:

Lord Jesus, I'm asking for your help. I need You today. Thank You for dying on the cross for every one of my sins. Please forgive me of all my sins and selfishness. By faith, I open the door of my life and invite you to come in. Jesus, I receive You as my Savior and Lord. I accept your gift of eternal life. Please, help me to life my life for you. Lord, I give my life to you; make me the kind of person You want me to be. Help me to love you with all my heart and to love others. Thank you for saving me from eternal destruction and adding my name to the Book of LIfe. Now, help me to live my life for you. Amen.

What you should do next (Stay on the narrow road)

While heaven is rejoicing at your faith in Jesus Christ (Luke 15:7), the enemy will continue to rear its ugly head. In 1 Peter 5:8, Satan is as a roaring lion, plotting against you. He wants to (1) rob you of God's Word and blessings, (2) kill your God given gifts, and (3) destroy your faith and walk in God. You must remain a believer, and strive to become a stronger one. You must do everything you can to grow in your love and faith in Christ. You must stay on the narrow road. In order to stay faithful to God, let me suggest three extremely important steps.

- **Begin to read the Word of God consistently.** It is the truth, the whole truth and nothing but the truth.

- **Find a good Bible believing church;** one that preaches the entire gospel and attend it regularly.
- **Find a person or a group and study the scriptures together.** Ask lots of questions. You're responsible to learn and grow in your understanding of Jesus and His Word.

Revelation 20:15
"Anyone not found written in the Book of Life was cast into the lake of fire"

Latest Books by the Author

Moments of Truth

Every one of us has moments of truth in life. These moments, crossroads, or chapters in life can be summed up in three words every Christian should know—three simple yet powerful words that ultimately define who we are today and what we will become in the future. Those words are love, forgiveness, and acceptance.

In *Moments of Truth*, author D.L. Formhals shares the story of inner struggle and his journey to love, forgiveness, and acceptance. Formhals presents stories and biblical principals in *Moments of Truth* that guide you to the knowledge that God will help you understand the past and deal with the future in a whole new way.

As oxygen, water, and food are to the human body, love, forgiveness, and acceptance are to the spirit. *Moments of Truth* will help you make a real, lasting positive change in your life *(Taken from the back cover).*

The Holy Spirit and Fire

Our Heavenly Father through His Word made a **PROMISE** to His people and to the world. That promise was a Messiah, the Savior. Jesus Christ was the fulfillment of that promise. As Jesus finished His earthly ministry He also made a promise to His followers; to send a comforter and a guide.

On the day of Pentecost Jesus' followers would come to realize the **PURPOSE** of the promise. As 120 believers gathered together in an upper room, they would receive the power of God to become true witnesses. When the Holy Spirit fell on each of them, like tongues of fire, the **PLAN** of God was unleashed. This book will help the reader understand the Biblical plan of the Lord to baptize all believers with ***The Holy Spirit and fire.***

Angels of God

A recent poll published in *Time Magazine* revealed that 69% of Americans believe in angels, and 46% believe they have a personal guardian angel. The word "angel" comes from the Greek word *aggelos;* which means "messenger." In this book you'll discover: 18 popular accounts of angels in scripture, the only 4 angelic names mentioned in the Bible, the 9 levels of angelic hierocracy, if guardian angels exist, the evil and fallen angels in the Bible, and several powerful stories about those who have entertained angelic beings.

Other Materials by the Author

Pastoral Ministry
101 Out Of This World Illustrations for Speakers (101 illustrations & stories)
Quotes to Quicken the Message (Over 1,200 quotes on all topics)
Ten Things Everyone Should Know (Lists of ten-Info. & reference)
101 On Fire Illustrations (101 illustrations & stories)

Church Ministry
The Holy Spirit and Fire (A Biblical guide to receiving the Baptism in the Holy Spirit)
12 Steps to Overcoming Sinful Habits In Life (12 Weeks: Sin/Habit/ Addiction)
Spiritual Assassins that Destroy Men (8 Week Bible Study on Men's Issues)

A Sure Foundation Leaders Guide (9 weeks: Leadership--new believer's course)

A Sure Foundation Student Workbook (9 weeks: new believer's course)

Being A Man of Valor (10 weeks: Bible study to encourage your men)

Applying God's Word to Your Life (7 weeks: Bible study on the Word of God)

Finding Your Motivational Gift (Leaders-Guide: All the gifts in Details-Script/PowerPoint)

Finding Your Motivational Gift Student Workbook (Fill in the blank notes)

Discovering Your Place in the Kingdom Of God (Leader & Student Guide — Spiritual Gifts)

Weight of the Lord (Leadership Edition: Book & PowerPoint. 6-week program weight loss program)

Weight of the Lord (Student Workbook)

Family Ministry

Bible For Bucks Proverbs (31 day Bible study compelling kids to read God's Word)

Moments of Truth (The power of love, forgiveness and acceptance)

Old, Wrinkled, and Closer to Heaven (Stories, jokes and a biblical perspective about old age)

Youth/Student Ministry

Amazing Young People (31 day student devotional)

Mini Messages For Youth Workers (30 ready to use sermons)

Motive8 Manual (Student Leadership)

Motive8 Student Workbook (Fill in the blank notes)

The Stupid Series Program (10 week series on the All-Time Stupid quotes in history)

The Race Is On Program (7 week Jr. High series on being faithful to God)

Radical Days With God (13 week student devotional)

Radical Discipleship (30 day intense discipleship on the words of Jesus)

Youth Files (A Biblical guide to all the youth in the Bible)

Quick Guide To Youth (A quick guide to all the youth in the bible)

Drama & Illustrated Messages

Christmas at Our House (A Christmas Sunday Morning Drama with script)

Drama for the Road (20 ready to use drama)

The Big Book of Illustrated Messages (10 Illustrated Message Scripts)

Creation Science/Evolution

Missing Think, The (30 proofs the earth is not millions of years old-Creation)

What about Dinosaurs? (What really happened to dinosaurs?)

Two World-Views a teaching on creation science and the Theory of Evolution (Audio/Script/PowerPoint).

CONTACT INFORMATION
ORDERS AND BOOKINGS

Website: DannyFormhals.com

Email: RevDLFormhals@gmail.com

Write: 2569 Rita Ave., McKinleyville, CA 95519